SPEED
LEARNING 101

*Train Your Brain to Learn More
and Faster*

Jeremy Allen

NEW GLOBE
Publishing

ISBN: 978-1-80283-859-6

Disclaimer Notice:

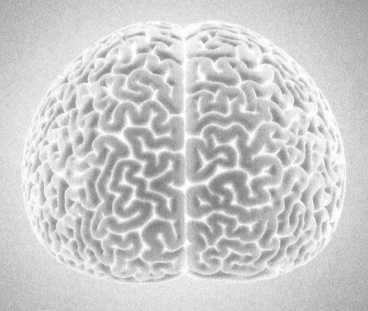

Table of Contents

1. INTRODUCTION

Almost every action we take is the product of prior learning, but for others, learning is only a practice performed in or connected with an educational context.

As kids, we learn to feed, pay attention, crawl, and walk, among other things, and as we grow into children and our bodies become more functional, we learn an astounding array of skills.

A lot of our learning happens at random during our lives, from new experiences, facts, and perspectives, such as reading a newspaper or watching a news show, talking with a friend or colleague, chance encounters, and unexpected experiences.

Many of our life experiences provide us with learning opportunities from which we can choose whether or not to learn. This type of experiential learning differs from more traditional approaches to learning, such as training, mentoring, coaching, and teaching, which all have some structure in the form of planned learning involving a facilitator.

Learning entails far more than just thinking: it entails the entire personality, including senses, emotions, instincts, convictions, values, and will. We will not learn if we do not have the desire to learn, and if we do learn, we will be changed somehow. If the learning does not affect us, it could be nothing more than a set of random thoughts that pass through our minds.

Learning through study is a long and arduous process that requires perseverance and commitment. Who wouldn't like to be able to learn the same things in half the time?

Speed learning is a group of learning strategies that aim to achieve higher learning rates without sacrificing comprehension or retention. It is similar to speed reading, but it also includes other types of learning such as observation, listening, discussion, questioning, and contemplation.

The general approach is to employ procedures or a series of techniques that have been demonstrated to provide a more effective path to achieving the same aim. Some methods date back to ancient times (for example, mnemonics), while others are more modern scientific studies (e.g., Forgetting Curves).

The mind processes information so quickly that you aren't even aware of it. Simply moving the eyes in a certain direction causes them to sense and recognize what is there.

Things aren't quite as smooth and fluid when we listen, though. Processing words and the meaning expressed by those words requires time and effort. Reading is a demanding task that requires a lot of mental energy for many people. Some people find it so taxing that they don't read at all.

So, why can't the text be processed in the same way as other items in our world are? We can, in fact, do it!

Since the eyes are closely attached to the brain, many people mistake them for brain extensions rather than distinct organs. According to scientists, visual information processing takes up to 65 percent of the brain.

If the eyes are the body's second most complex organ, the brain is the most complex. Many believe it to be the most complex structure globally, surpassing planets, stars, and even airplanes. The brain drives every thinking, behavior, memory, feeling, and experience we have in the world.

Within minutes of reading any of the pages, you can double or even triple your current reading speed, and you can speed up even further after practicing the additional suggestions.

There's no doubt that if you put in the effort, you'll be able to read a 200-page book in an hour!

Reading and comprehension go hand in hand, so you'll learn to develop your comprehension as well as your reading speed. After all, the aim of reading more quickly is to gain more knowledge. What good is speed reading if we can't understand and remember what we're reading? It's not speed-reading if you don't improve your comprehension.

If you purchased this book, you're probably eager to learn how to learn quickly. After examining how our brains learn and remember, we will take action in the following chapters. Get ready to learn faster than you ever imagined possible!

2. BENEFITS OF SPEED LEARNING

Speed learning has tremendous benefits for everyone in everyday life, especially for business people, students, and everyone who reads a lot.

With so much material bombarding us daily, spending a little time learning techniques for quicker reading makes sense. Consider zipping through your inbox in half the time or skimming through your friends' social media posts and reacting quickly.

However, since speed reading techniques take time to learn and you're already busy, you might be wondering why you should bother adding yet another "must do" thing to your

To-Do list. Let's take a look at some of the reasons why you should learn to speed read.

Empowerment: You are at ease wherever you are

Every day, people judge you by the words that come out of your mouth. If you're at a business conference, you'll be hesitant to present your point of view if you're not certain of your evidence. Reading (and understanding what you're reading) provides you with information that can be converted into wisdom.

You feel at ease with your peers in social settings. They are aware of your existence. However, at events, you must have plenty to chat about. And when others are debating a subject, you need to weigh in. Speed reading the news — from global affairs to gossip — provides you with a plethora of topics for social chit-chat.

Money: you will be able to find better jobs

Money represents independence and protection for you and your family. Awareness is force, whether you want to advance in your current job or get a better job.

If you want to advance in your career, you must stand out. Online courses and structured professional education will assist you in accomplishing this. Obtaining a bachelor's or advanced degree makes you more appealing to prospective employers in general. Similarly, holding a degree or credential that those vying for a promotion lack raises your value to your boss. This improved worth translates into a higher salary.

Speed reading will help you enhance your education by easily handling all of the coursework required for further education.

Improved personality traits: you'll gain trust

How comfortable are you communicating with your boss? You can feel assured that you can answer his or her questions if you understand your business, its rivals, the current market, and financial news. You'll be able to confidently make recommendations for your department and the company as a whole.

What about expressing your viewpoint to someone you know would disagree with you? Are you sure you want to do that? If you're well-read, you'll feel at ease in both situations: learning to speed read is important.

Improved memory: you'll remember things more quickly

Speed learning improves your comprehension through rapid reading. You can remember a subject or fact if you understand why it is relevant.

Your enhanced memory will benefit you in other aspects of your life as well. Since memory is a component of creativity, you will discover that you are more creative in all aspects of your life.

More opportunities: you can improve your learning capacity

Do you have difficulty concentrating on tasks? Speed reading skills will also help you concentrate. You'll be more interested in everything you learn, and with your increased imagination, you'll be ready to further your education. More and better prospects arise as a result of your increased schooling.

Sophistication: your reasoning abilities will increase

The neuroplasticity of your brain can be affected by speed reading. It aids in the formation of new neural connections in your brain. This means that not only will your imagination change, but so will your thinking.

Feel less stressed because concentration is a meditative ability

Do you have trouble focusing on tasks? Since information bombards us in so many forms, many people attempt to multitask to get more done. This results in disjointed focus and overall inefficiency. Speed reading helps you to concentrate. This, like meditation, relieves tension.

Increased ambition: you will be motivated to advance in your career.

You will become more ambitious if you have a stronger memory, new imagination, enhanced cognitive skills, and the ability to concentrate on tasks. Your universe is expanding. You'll be eager to advance up the career ladder in your profession.

Thought leadership: the more you know, the more innovative you will be

Leaders in every profession who are thought leaders innovate. They are creative, and they apply what they know. Combining and integrating non-obvious ideas and objects is critical for creativity and a key component of the creative-thinking process. It engages your imagination and thus activates your creativity engine, in addition to your ability to reframe problems.

Speed learning could lead you to the next billion-dollar idea — and the opportunity to put that idea into action.

Improved problem-solving abilities

All face difficulties. The subconscious mind can solve them. The conscious mind solves problems at a rate of approximately 100–150 miles per hour. Meanwhile, our subconscious is racing at about 100,000 m.p.h.

You can stream more information to your subconscious mind by studying at a faster pace. Your subconscious can solve your problems with more detail.

3. HOW WE LEARN

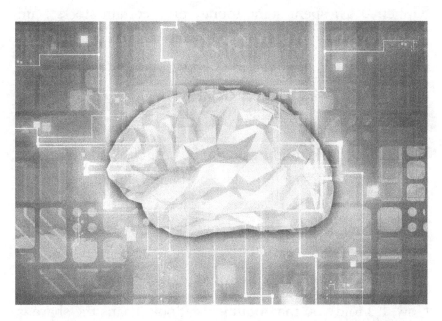

To process any new information coming into your brain, it must be deciphered and understood for it to stay locked in your mind's eye. Your brain processes information and endeavors to form patterns in order to comprehend the messages that it receives. When you are in a state of confusion, this simply means that your brain is working overtime trying to find a link between what you already know and the new information. A breakthrough is lingering no matter what the subject. Your mind links together what you don't know (have just seen/learned from somewhere) to concepts that you already have an understanding of.

Let me provide an example. At this point, I am learning how the stock market works because I want to eventually trade. I have begun paper trading, which simply means that I am looking at the stock market and seeing what may have happened if I spent some money on a certain stock. I am simulating the actual act but not using real money.

"The stock looks bullish, so I would apply a bull call spread to minimize my initial investment and still be able to buy the number of contracts I want."

If someone knows nothing about how options and the stock market work, this would mean nothing. I am sure we have been in a situation when information was given to us at some point in our lives. However, we have no reference point whatsoever in our brain to link concepts to comprehend the situation we are faced with.

Now, if I told you that a bullish outlook means the share is going to rise (bulls raise their horns in an up sweeping manner, bears hold their paws in a downwards manner, so bearish means it will fall), and that a call option is an option you buy when the share rises. A spread means I'm buying and writing call options. You could understand mostly what the statement is saying. People who don't know the exact terminology for the share market would turn around and ask me what it means to write options; I'm simply saying selling options to guarantee stock at another price. Everybody understands what it means to buy and sell.

By explaining the concept above in 'fundamental universal concepts,' your knowledge in any area can grow.

The point is to understand what is going on in a subject, and it is based on what you already understand, so comparing yourself to other students will serve you no purpose. Grappling with insecurities of comparing yourself with others will change your belief system and your 'internal representation.' The simple act of dwelling on your perceived limitations will alter your mindset and lead you to failure.

Any successful person is only in competition with themselves and never in competition with their environment or others. Successful people will adapt a strategy and follow a plan. They will then extend this action into every area of their life and not just concentrate it in one field only.

Fortitude means to gain courage in pain and adversity. Courage, endurance, patience, forbearance, tenacity and bravery are but a few of the virtues of the discipline of fortitude. Fortitude is the power by which we gain mastery over experience. It is the ability to not panic in situations but to gain mastery of true responsibility. Fortitude is the building block of true leaders. It is when your experience is greater than the demands of the lesson.

To have convictions of your beliefs, have emotions of integrity, and know how to meet your own needs; these are all functions of leadership and success. So with each lesson, if you gain the experience in a positive attitude. This positive attitude will be the fuel for all future success.

There is no such thing as failure, there is only feedback

By the successful students that I have interviewed and known, I have gained much insight into how they deal with their fear. You must grow in fortitude and adversity to fear and never to strengthen fear. Your ultimate result will always depend on how you deal with fear. Make emotions your friends with messages. Each friend has a message for your system. Listen to the message wisely. If it screams fear, you are spending your valued time in contemplation when you study, not on the facts you need to absorb. The ones who seem so smart, failure is simply the act of not getting back on the horse, these students dance with fear; they know it exists. However, they use it as a sign that they must prepare, never to somehow drive them.

Before you can seriously study, you must have your psychology under control. You cannot change error at an intellectual level when the problem is emotional. Fear is an emotion, and it must be changed at an emotional level. You must do exercises to overcome your fear. To learn to direct it in ways that you can control. Never to be consumed by it.

The simple concept of linking info you don't know to info you do know is the basis of learning anything. Every person on this planet, I guarantee you, knows something you don't; the same goes for you and everyone else!

Very basic, you might say, I cannot tell you the amount of time I see people studying and never using tools like metaphors, pictures, stories to grasp the underlying concept. If you are trying to work out if it is a question, then it is not the answer you want to memorize. It is the process to get you the answer you want to be locked in your mind so you can repeat the process any time it's needed.

Why not help your brain and give it the links it needs to store the info, then give it the info.

My friend Mark was a pro at this, it saved him so much time whenever he was learning or teaching me a new formula, system, or any information for that matter. He would describe it using any props he could find, using his hands, drawing, making the most complicated things at first glance, look as simple as reading the alphabet out, one letter at a time! When the info was linked directly to things, I totally understood, which could be as simple as the concept of 'freezing water makes it expand.'

Learning intellectually is using only one resource that you have. If you conscript all your resources, you will use your visual brain, auditory brain, metaphors, and tools that will embed the information into the parts of your brain's filing system for quick, easy retrieval.

Different ways to learn

The way a typical classroom is set up is you sit at a desk and follow the teachers' presentation for hours, days, weeks, then are examined on it, and they give you some references and send you on your way.

A good friend of mine took some classes with me, during class she would never take many notes, just listen and process. I on the other hand had to scribble down everything and hope for the best when revision time came along. I would hope that I could remember what he/she was on about when it came time to revise for the exam and make sense of my notes. This girl, I thought was amazing, she didn't take that much time to study for exams; she went in remembering everything the lecturer said during class. I will explain exactly how this was done, and how it can be repeated.

Practice makes perfect right? I defiantly believe this to be true; repetition is the key of any skill. These are the answers any great sports star, movie star or professional would answer to the question "how are you so skilled?" However practicing the wrong way will not get you to where you want to go. We all have different personalities, different ways of looking at the world, and processing it. Psychologists have listed ways to learn, some people are better than others in these different paths I am about to describe...

The example of my friend above was that of a great auditory learner, which meant that what ever she heard would make complete sense to her. The lecturer talking away was all she needed to learn. I on the other hand am a much more visual and kinesthetic learner, I need to picture what is going on. I work much better when diagrams are being shown to me, when I can feel and experience the new information in my mind.

The great thing for my friend is because of the normal 'classroom setup,' she was able to practice each day, anytime she was in class, her 'talent' or 'nature' of learning was expanding, which meant getting a better time. She appeared to be a genius because of all the correct (for her) practice she had.

Whenever I focused on learning information and joining new bits together, I make sure it is done in an auditory and kinesthetic way rather than sitting like a stunned mullet in class, hoping it will somehow be fed to my subconscious mind and will pop right out to me when ever I need it. Because I now focus on this simple transition of learning, I 'practice' only to discover new things; hence, I am getting better and better at it. This is a definite change of hitting that brick wall all day long!

So you are hopefully asking, "how do I really know if I learn better by Visual, Auditory or kinesthetic means. I have developed a simple test you can do right now to confirm any feelings you might have to what is the best way for you to learn.

Discovering how you learn

Knowing what is best for you to begin continually practicing is extremely helpful for learning and can easily cut studying time considerably. To find this out, fill in the form below, where under each heading, you write as many adjectives as you can think of for 2 minutes under each column. The longest list will give you an idea of your preferred learning and processing mode. When you find out the answer, next time you are struggling and frustration sets in when trying to learn something, have it explained to you in a way you know it will sink in.

4. HOW MEMORY WORKS

The mind does not store information in slots on a shelf like a library. It merely stores many representations of what was witnessed. Take, for example, viewing your aunt's face; the image is not stored in one part of the brain. So when you need to recall any type of image, your interpretation is a representation through your own meanings and feelings expelled. If your aunt was a caring, loving, funny person, the image would have associations with these emotions. A warm, soft image could be drawn from your memory. If, on the other hand, a horrible, evil aunt graces your family, you will conjure up a hard-looking dark, restricted face. Another interesting fact is that the face based on negative experiences will be harder to recall later on. This image does not excite the pleasure center of the brain. The part of the brain that makes it easier for you to remember things

Memory and images are associated with the emotional part of the brain, so when memorizing, it would be advised that you elicit emotion for clarity and faster recall.

Studying for exams or 'storing' the information needed to excel in any subject usually begins on the wrong foot. The example of remembering your aunt's face can be easily related to your initial reaction to any workload that needs to be totally understood in detail. When you consciously start making up reasons why you can't learn such as bad teaching, horrible layout, hhhuuugggeeee awful work load etc, etc... This will put you in a state where your mind with much pain associated with the subject that sub consciously, and a considerable amount will reduce your memory retention. Not to mention a major decrease in your motivation to continue learning what the subject has to offer. Many people would say that you have failed before you have even begun.

Another person cannot make you feel any emotion; they can only trigger what is already in your internal reference system. Another person can not make you enjoy certain course material because we all have different goals, varying desires and past experiences. Even though all humans have the same needs, we meet those needs in totally different ways. However, the good news has the power to control your feelings, beliefs and reasons why you like different things. How you choose to interpret the world, and your surroundings are 100% totally in your control!

To begin retaining any material, we need to use technology that we can turn on at any time to see a subject as we want to see it. Once you master it, this technology will ensure that you enjoy the weeks, days, and hours before any exam! Wow, what a thought, I know. Once you master this technique, then the subconscious does not control you any longer. No matter how the environment presents itself, you will strengthen your resolve and use setbacks as fuel.

Ok, Ok, enough bragging about it! This Tool has a name, and it is called the Calibrator. Pretty fancy name, huh? There are four steps to follow, and the end result is that the quality of your life amid things which could seem super boring, seem useless, or seem a waste of time, can be so easily converted into fun and enthusiasm as YOU can now conjure a way to 'feel' that way and not how the environment orders you to feel.

Draw a horizontal line with markings from -10 to +10. The first step is simply just to mark on the graph how you feel about studying where -10 is the utter pits, where you would rather roll around in cow dung than bake in the sun and breath in what you have plastered all over your body. Then +10 is where you would rather study and wrap your mind around this work than get a date with your absolute dream guy or gal and excel far beyond what you think you are capable of.

-10 -9 -8 -7 -6 -5 -4 -3 -2 -1 0 1 2 3 4 5 6 7 8 9 10

The odds are that you will be in the negative numbers on your initial feelings about a subject in which you know deep down you can achieve much more. Keep in mind the Calibrator, as I said, can be used for any emotion you may have for any subject matter you know. It is good for you, but you just hate doing it! I use this tool on myself all the time, for example, getting up early in the morning to go for a walk or a jog. I know consciously it really is good for me; however, when it's cold out, and my bed feels so warm, I can hear the wind howling, and the sun isn't even up yet, so why should I be up (that would be my initial thought) therefore I would mark a -7 on the graph.

The truth is that the human brain sees things for not what they are but always worse than reality. Once you begin on the negative side of the graph, the initial feeling is "stacked" with feelings that follow and many people somehow to turn the experience into one of the worst in their lives. This leads to feelings of desperation, thinking there is no way out and that life is so hard and I might as well drop out! Fail, or settle for a scrape-through the mark. The difference between people like this and those who always get top marks is a simple fact that consciously they see where they are and NEVER make it worse than it is, hence picking a mark on the scale assures you where you are, many students I have found over the years seem to go around in circles. This is not to say that feelings of "hope" could elevate your score on the graph.

Hope is not solid but flimsy, and the emotions are easily allowed to drop down again into the negative category. The answer to this is to know exactly where you are by visualizing it on paper and a graph.

The second step is simply to consciously decide what feelings and emotions you wish to experience with the work you KNOW need to be done! Preferably use your conscious mind to decide the best emotions you have lived once before to give you the result you seek. So, choose in advance the experience you are committed to achieving rather than playing out the same boring subconscious thoughts which lead you to the same result every time. Your usual pattern of thought has never given you the results you wanted, so begin to change your pattern of thought.

The third step is even easier. Simply record a numerical value to the quality of experience you are committed to having. The advantage of this step is to now have a place you want to be, in a concentrating working environment, where time no longer exists, and all the energy normally wasted on worrying and stress turns into super focus and resources to understand work are brought effortlessly to the surface. Once you have marked on the Calibrator what your goal is, you must develop a…

(Forth Step) … simple plan; I know, I know…May seem impossible, and you might remark what a simple tool with no defining purpose. However, the simplicity of this tool is the genius of it, you see your mind is controlled directly by questions.

You may begin to doubt this remark; however, think about it when you think, ponder, decide, judge something, try to manipulate or care for someone. Whatever is going through your mind, it is just a simple process of asking and answering questions. Again you might say that is not true but give it a test right now. Let your mind wonder, when I first tried this, I thought about a tropical island, then trying to remember if I turned the iron off, then about maybe my dream car or house, then what I'm having for dinner this evening!

The secret to success and intelligence is to be able to see the fine distinctions within our environment, including how the mind works. To recognize patterns is to solve the mystery. I want you to see the pattern and realize that all thoughts are brought about by either conscious (someone asking you) or subconscious (you asking yourself) questions, and every thought is simply an answer to a question. I'm sure you have all heard the saying, ask a stupid question, get a stupid answer; this implies directly how I once viewed how to tackle a huge workload. I would come up with thoughts (sub-conscious answers) that did not help me out because after inspection of my own mind. I found my questions were something like "what is better than doing this right now?" or "I really have lots of time to go through this work, don't I?" these questions would give me answers to getting out of the work or finding reasons, excuses why I wouldn't get off my behind! My favorite thought was "Why now, why me in this class?" type of question. These thoughts scramble your brain and lead you around in circles and defiantly not to the mark you want on your straight-line graph.

It has been postulated that trying the same approach over and over again is simply a definition of insanity!

Here is the good news! The fourth step is achieved very easily by moving from your subconscious to your conscious mind. This is where you direct the questions and are not driven by the standard feelings that always crop up because of whatever meanings you have given to results in the past.

First, just a quick remark: The subconscious means well, it really isn't trying to sabotage you. It runs just as a computer does on a program. The only difference is your mind is a SUPER COMPUTER. The subconscious mind is trying to get you away from 'pain' because let's face it, there are probably many more fun things to do than study!

However, the subconscious has no ideas of how much Pain you will be in when it's the night before the exam, and you feel nowhere near confident enough to have the absolute pleasure you deserve walking out of that room right after!

Therefore we simply take back control and re-program our subconscious mind by using tools by our conscious creation.

There are hundreds of these types of questions you could ask. Rather than committing to an experience (say what was once an awful lecture) expecting pain and getting it, you are asking questions to redirect your focus, and with the addition of each of these changes in perception, you will find that the experience is immediately enhanced. It focuses on the conscious mind and the language used, which programs the subconscious mind and thus programs your emotions.

The trick is to move up two or three notches at a time; don't move from -6 to a +4 in one go and with one question. It won't stick. Simply move up the scale, asking yourself, even when you can't think of a question, "what could I do..." to feel a -2 then 0 (neutral), +2 and so on.

Your Brain and Memory

A thought is conjured up when a neuron's firing associated with that thought occurs by conscious stimulation. Or in simpler terms, when you know, something must be remembered, and you tell yourself to do so! Memory is when that neuron causes a neighboring neuron to spark simply by proximity. This causes the receptor that normally lies deep within that cell to reach the cell's outer surface. This occurs so that if the thought is conjured up again within a relatively short time within a few hours, the connection between the 2 neurons will be a lot easier. The more times this 'thought' occurs, the stronger the bond or the stronger the memory will be until it becomes permanently etched in your mind. When you learn something new, you should re-enforce it within a short time frame other wise it will be a lot harder to recall. Everyone has heard this before.

What memory is not encouraged or committed are mere words on a page. The reason why you don't forget that the Eiffel Town is in Paris or why people will never forget an old friend who has died many years ago is because of Associated EMOTIONS! Combining some words or something you heard with excitement will cause the memory to stick in your mind. The reason is that excitement is brought on by a surge of unique neuro-transmitters that increase the firing rate of neurons in certain parts of the brain; hence those permanent connections between neurons will occur much faster.

Exciting emotions increase the intensity of perception. Positive emotions also boost the long term potential, so events that happen in such a state are much more likely to be remembered

Things can be viewed a lot easier as step by step or in 'chunks' rather than by one whole mess of knowledge that has to be instilled permanently in your mind just before an exam. This perception is what you want in order to see the 'nitty gritty' of your work. The steps that lead to the larger picture will need to be totally understood before examined upon.

Other techniques include listening to music reciting the main points of whatever topic you are focusing on, which empowers you. For example, the Rocky movie theme or any of your favorites would instill excitement, perseverance, courage, joy, and other motivating and empowering emotions. Many students focus on what they don't know and what resources they don't have!

Positive emotions or pleasure associated with learning will remain a longer time than negative emotions and feelings.

Pegs and Calls to action

A fundamental concept that will serve you very well is to know that the mind always thinks in pictures, metaphors and analogies. Starting to apply this simple technique will dramatically increase your awareness and understanding of how your mind was designed for you to learn! Basic word association is an age-old memory technique. I have found that in many exams, I have needed to remember:

- A list of things

- steps to a procedure

- An order of how something's fits.

And I undertook a memory course years ago to which I still use what I learned. The course is by a gentleman named Kevin Trudeau and is called Mega Memory.

This list is called a pegs list and all I have to do, even to this day, is 'attach' a list to my pegs, and it is locked in. Not to be forgotten, whether it is a shopping list or anything which would be needed to be recalled during an exam, it is still one of the best ways in which to legally cheat for any paper! I will first show you:

- What the list is

- Why each number has a referral to the item on that list

- How to never forget the list

- Finally, how to attach whatever needs to be remembered onto the list and

- Be able to be recalled the info at any time need be for your next exam!

Pegs list

1. Tree

2. Light switch

3. STOOL

4. Car

5. Glove

6. Gun

7. Dice

8. Skate

9. Cat

10. Bowling Ball

11. Goal Posts

12. Eggs

13. Witch

14. Ring

15. Paycheck

16. Candy

17. Magazine

18. Voting Booth

19. Golf Club

20. Cigarettes

Basic word association is the linking together in a logical fashion something you know and something you don't know. Next time you need to recall a list instead of trying to remember what goes first, second and so on, the particular order in which a list or any order of something which must be committed to memory are defined not by the numbers one to twenty. It is by pictures which are how your mind works! The numbers will now become pictures, and remembering what goes with which number is as easy as recalling an associated image. As shown:

NOTE: THE GREATER THE DETAIL IN YOUR MIND'S EYE OF THESE PICTURES, THE LONGER AND EASIER IT WILL STICK THERE!

So, below I will describe each image that will now become your number 1 to number 20. Please stick with me on this...I promise the results will absolutely speak for themselves.

Just imagine the images described below – next to each corresponding number. The numbers 1 to 20 will change from just 'numbers' into pictures. Before are small descriptions on how to do just that. We need to find a common theme between the number and the picture described below.

Tree: The image conjured up here is a that a tree Trunk looks like the number 1 Light Switch: Light switch is made of 2 words, 2 positions (on/off), (light, dark) Stool: Has 3 Legs

Car: 4 Wheels, 4 doors, 4WD

Glove: 5 fingers for each glove

Gun: 6 Shooter, then someone could be 6 Foot under!

Dice: Adding opposite sides of a dice always equals 7, Casino; "Lucky No 7!" Skate: Simply Rhymes, Skate in figure 8, inline or roller skates, 8 wheels Cat: Has 9 lives!

Bowling Ball: 10 Pins, 10 points for a strike

Goal Post: It looks like an 11... 11 players on a soccer or football team

Eggs: A dozen eggs is 12

Witch: Unlucky Black Friday the 13th

Ring: 14 Carat gold ring, Valentines Day 14th Feb

Paycheck: Start work when you are 15, get paid middle of the month on the 15th

Candy: Sweet 16!

Magazine: Seventeen is an actual name of a magazine.

Voting Booth: must be 18 years old to Vote

Golf Club: the 19th hole, is the term given after a round of 18 holes is done

Cigarettes: 20 'cigarettes' in a Pack

This list can be easily committed to memory by going over the list in your mind when your driving, cooking, during the ads on T.V or going for a Jog. Simply say to yourself, "Five is Glove, because five fingers fits a glove"..." Six is a gun because a six-shooter can put you six feet under"..." Twelve is eggs since when buying eggs they always come by the dozen" etc. Committing to memory why each image goes with what number is most important.

If you think you need some special ability to store this list in your mind, let me tell you a story. This list was taught to mentally disadvantaged people of all ages and conditions, and in the same way, it is taught to students now. During a totally independent study, the test subjects not only committed the list to memory but when called back unannounced months and years later. The tree was still number one, and cigarettes were still the number 20.

I undertook the memory course when I was in my young teens and still to this day serves me when needed. However, this is just the first part; once this list becomes locked in and it will, you need to know how to use it to whatever your own 'list' will be for an exam.

As you know, the mind works in pictures and metaphors, or relations between those pictures. We want to now stick your 'list' to that of your new 'numbers.' I feel I can show this best with an example. If I wanted to commit to heart the 7 main elements of any story. Every story follows a formula that all movie script writers and novelists follow.

These are the steps that writers follow:

1.   Desire: The desire becomes the driving force behind the main characters' present behavior.

2.   Problem: The problem or need comes up, and the character unbecomingly always focuses on what they think is their real need; however, their folly does not become evident until…

3.   Opponent: …The opponent shows up, and in many cases, the opponent is themselves or some external 'evil' person. As always the bigger the opponent, the bigger the hero.

4.   Plan: The main character comes up with a plan to deal with the opponent. He must have his outcome clear in his mind.

5.   Battle: The 'battle' scene is in all great memorable movies, whether it be a battle scene with themselves, their loved one, a whole army, or an evil opponent!

6.   Self-revelation: The main character has a change of perception, a realization, and forms new values or traits. Usually, universal traits such as courage, love, caring and honesty come into his perception after his battle.

7.   Equilibrium: The character finally develops a new belief system with new values and meanings developed as a result of the major lesson he has learned by overcoming his opponents. The 'Real' need is finally fulfilled, and "life will never be the same again" or "they lived happily ever after."

I mentioned earlier that we must stick this new list of data to our 'pegs' list or now known as our new numbers 1 to 20. We have to convert these words, which will automatically come forth from your brain when viewed a few times with pictures attached. To 'stick' things that must be remembered to our list...Or in our memory, we need very strong 'super glue,' so when time goes by, and we learn more, it doesn't get pushed out!

This has been tried and tested with many factors during experiments under various conditions. The conclusion is that the best way to remember anything is to use MASSIVE ACTION as that glue. By this, I mean that we must use our new list turned into pictures and have Crazy, Huge, Unrealistic, Stupid action(s) combining those two pictures. The steps (in detail are explained below).

Step 1: For the first on the list, Desire, we need a picture; the easiest way to do this is to change the word into a picture that has nothing to do with its meaning, only with the sound of the word. Breaking it up into its syllables always does the trick and allows more detailed pictures. So desire becomes de and sire.

Pictures for any list come totally from your imagination. The first image which pops in my mind is a Tea cup (since Tea sounds like de), but adding the most detail possible will make it stay; therefore, it is no ordinary tea cup sitting on a bench. I'm imagining a very pretty tea cup covered in wild bright, vibrant flowers, such as yellow, purple and green, with a teabag whizzing round and round in scorching hot boiling tea; the cup is on a saucer spinning about unpredictably and could at anytime spill all over me!

For the word sounding of sire. I instantly imagine a King, sitting on his huge gold throne, in his entire royal outfit, including the royal jewels. He looks pleased with himself as it is 4:00 pm, and he is looking at the object of his desire, a cup of tea in a saucer as described above. He can taste the tea going into his mouth.

The more senses you use to describe your scene, the greater the memory. Use visual, sensory, auditory, sensory, kinesthetic and gustatory methods to form emotion.

This being the 1st thing you need to remember, it must be 'glued' to your image of a tree (or your new number 1). To remember this as being the number 1 thing to remember, I use my imagination to have the king sitting on his throne under a tree. When first doing this exercise, my initial thoughts were how silly it seemed, and you might think all this time is wasted making up wacky images and pegging them when I could use repetition. In actual fact, the required knowledge will stay in your mind for a longer period of time it will take MUCH shorter time then continually trying to drum it into your mind and having it stay there.

In my crazy mind I would envision a tree, yes with a face, sitting by the sire with arms thrown around the king or sire and the sire sitting with tea. With an image like this conjured up in my mind as stupid as it seems, it works like a charm every time. As an exercise you should peg the rest of the 'elements of a story' to your new numbers list.

Remembering Formulas

Formulas can also be remembered by a story. You may perceive that trying to remember another story is cumbersome. However, remembering stories is the way into the subconscious mind. This will allow you to memorize anything for a longer time. The power of stories is greater than you may think, you can always remember a great story. People never get halfway through telling a hilarious story, made them laugh and then forget the ending. This is because of the EMOTION attached to the story, the laughter, the anger, the sadness...etc, allows them to remember the whole story in absolute detail.

That is the power of your mind when its working optimally with full imagination and being told with every part of you, not just what words you speak but what your body is also saying. More importantly, what you are feeling.

Imagine such a story to remember your formulas, halleluiah!! Maths will actually be fun. You will never struggle to remember things again!

Recalling Formulas has been a nightmare for many students I have encountered, Including ME! But grasping this simple continuation of what was discussed above can help you see that it really is not a big drama at all. To prove this to you, lets use the example below

The formula can be turned into a story with a little imagination

Here goes...Some time in the future (N)elly the rap artist has grown wearing huge gold chains and a massive jersey and using his walking stick to now plot around (.), leaving a trail. He comes to a square hedge with huge roots changing the terrain below his feet ( ), bending over to see below the hedge are 2 beagle dogs (d2) standing on their hind legs with monocles and top hats, and in their black vests, they are taking out and examining treasure maps where(X) marks the spot. Nelly makes his way through the hedge and over the roots to speak to the dogs who are speaking in old English accents. All three look in the distance to see a cat skating (number 8 on the memorized pegs list above) towards them wearing huge novelty gloves (number 5) "I say, I say", says one dog to the others "shouldn't we be chasing him, isn't it our duty?" Before the others can answer the Cat swipes them, they duck (__), and Nelly falls, grabbing one of the Beagles treasure maps ((x), times sign) to prevent the hard fall. It is not strong enough, and it rips from the dogs' vest and the other dog lifts his leg and pees (v, from the sound of the word) on Nelly. Go over the story once more, and that is all it takes to remember this formula above.

While I was writing this section, the great thing is that I do not need to have to be proud of it, as long as I can recall the story in my head. The actions of the story change my state (I am now happy making up the story and laughing at its absurdity); it's locked in for any exam, one of the best ways to legally 'cheat'!

Memory techniques, no matter what type, be it substitutions and associative links, no matter how humiliating and child-like, after all, it was when you were a child where your greatest learning capabilities lie.

Memory has no pride, no ego to stroke, and feels no shame, allowing us to be labeled 'respectable adults' to be kids again! We can use these techniques to remember anything, even people's names, like recalling a famous American President "Theodore Roosevelt" by picturing a stuffed teddy bear wearing a belt made out of red roses (Teddy Rosebelt). It's the best resource we have because there is no need to be self-conscious; nobody knows what we are thinking.

"We lose much of the power of the brain if we

consider ourselves too elegant to accept

help through associations, Visualization, Its

how the memory functions."

Medical Professor Wolf Seufert

Mnemonics

A mnemonic is another great way to remember course material. Mnemonics are often verbal or sometimes laid out like rhymes would be and are often used to remember lists. Mnemonics rely on repetition to remember facts and associations between easy-to-remember images set in concrete in your mind's eye and lists of anything you need to recall for a test.

To have this way of remembering work as effectively as possible, each item you want to remember must be associated with something that is permanently stuck in your long-term memory. The method I'm getting to is using Loci.

Loci is simply the name for location, and this location, I feel, is best explained by my list of items of certain locations in a structured path. What I mean is this.

Close your eyes and imagine your bedroom, in a circle from the front door list 5 to 10 items until you reach the door again, all from memory E.g., For my room:

I Have a List of 7 items (shown above). Now all that must be done is have fun using your imagination as vividly and crazily and as absurd as possible.

To make the illustration easy, we will use the simple example of remembering a shopping list; this is also a great way to practice using the mnemonic technique. The first item will be potatoes, so you could imagine something like a huge Mr. Potato character snoring while sleeping lying down in your draws; when you pull open the draw, he jumps up yells at you for waking him up!

REMEMBER: THE MORE VIVID COLORFUL AND CRAZY THE IMAGE THE MORE IT WILL 'STICK' FOR A MUCH LONGER TIME!

The second item to remember for the sake of this exercise is washing powder. For this item, I could see myself using my wardrobe as a washing machine covered in powder and using a hose to splash water all over my clothes in the hope they will look bright and smell great. Don't you love the smell of washing powder? Remember I said vividly! Using more than just the visual aspect of our senses is a great way to lock that item into our long-term memory bank.

This is a simple list. To remember items that require a lot more detail, I will use the First Amendment of the American constitution and item number 3, (the window of my room).

Amendment 1: Freedom of religion, Speech and the press; Right of Assembly

Locus 3. Window:

Imagine a Bishop in his full clerical outfit, holding a newspaper all rolled up and bashing it against the window, wanting to come in because he cannot stand the woman next to him, who is making a loud political speech through a megaphone. Next to her, a small group of protestors has assembled, cheering and waving big brightly colored signs.

Now you have locked in an intensely detailed description all by recalling what you always knew, that the window is next to the Wardrobe!

"Imagination grows by exercise! And is more powerful than anything conceived my man to this date, so why not use yours to serve you." -Anonymous

Different types of Mnemonics

You don't have to rely on Loci, or vivid images as I showed earlier, if you tend to be better at storing information, hearing things (auditory) or feeling how things would be (kinesthetic) for example. There are many great other ways to use Mnemonics to serve yourself that don't just rely on Visual stimulation.

Rhymed Mnemonics are as old as time itself; however, many people don't seem to be used to store data in your brain anymore. Examples of Rhymed Mnemonics include " I before E, except after C. Or "thirty Days hath September, April, June and November."

Another Class of Mnemonics is based on Acronyms; this is where each letter of a stand out word represents a list of facts that relate to a common theme:

Quite a while ago, I heard an acronym for N.R.M.A, which in Australia is like the Auto Club to help stranded motorists for those overseas readers. This service provides people who drive to wherever you are and your broken down car is and help get you on your way again. It sticks in my mind simply because it sounded funny. "No Real Mechanic Available" is what many people thought from experience using the service. In my mind, I found it very amusing. Proof that is adding leverage to any memory technique, whether humorous, is under stress, pressure, etc... It is up to you, so why not leave the stressful, very unproductive ways, which make you, hate studying behind and adapt ways to 'lock' memories in place by using funny even rude ways, I know one thing as an example... I'll never forget my PIN!

Acrostic Style Techniques is the technical term for using a silly sentence and having each first letter of each word in that sentence stand for something else. The notes on the Treble Clef for those music buffs are EGBDF and can be remembered by the sentence. "Every Good Boy Deserves Fruit." If you want the kids to rot their teeth, swap Fruit for Fudge!

Codes are also a great way to store info in your mind in preparation for an exam and have been used during Wars and to communicate between individuals to disguise what was being said, so only the intended people would get the message. Codes can be very complicated and very easy to decipher. The Verse

" How I wish I could recapture pi.

Eureka! Cried the great inventor.

Christmas pudding, Christmas pie

Is at the problems very center"

Allows anyone to appear super smart, how? The Verse above, once deciphered, will give you the value of pi, (Л) to 21 places, each word represents a digit, and the number of letters in that word is the numerical value of that digit, (how = 3, I = 1, wish = 4, and so on). Hence Pi: (3.141592653589793223846) can be remembered by anyone!

5. SPEED READING TECHNIQUES

Space reading

In order for these techniques to make sense, it helps to understand an important feature of the eye. The eye can process an image or object both as a whole and as a collection of individual parts. When looking at a friend's face, for example, the eyes and mind process the face as a whole rather than looking at individual parts, such as eyes, mouth, nose, and other minute features. This allows you to recognize the friend immediately. At the same time, if you wanted to focus on the individual features, you could do that as well.

Though, what would happen if you did focus on a single feature of your friends, such as an eyelash, nostril, or dimple? Narrowing vision to such a minute detail would hinder the ability to recognize the person. Such a restricted focus would require scanning other parts of the face and then putting all those parts together to recognize that individual.

This is how most of us read; we narrow our focus to each word or letter. Much like understanding a face, this process forces us to read bit by bit—letter by letter or word by word—to absorb any significant meaning. If we are distracted or our mind wanders, we miss the meaning of the entire sentence or paragraph and must start over.

This is not an effective way to read since, as you now know, the eyes and mind can see and process much more in a single glance. The solution, therefore, is to not focus on single words but rather to expand visual awareness and see groups of words at one time. This is the natural way the mind absorbs information from sight.

There are two ways to look at groups of words. The first method, which I call Space Reading®, will be covered in this chapter.

You're probably wondering, how the heck will looking at the spaces between words improve reading speed and comprehension? Understanding the answer helps to understand how I discovered the technique.

Since the mind and eyes can process information from sight extremely fast, I thought, why should reading be any different? I began thinking, there's got to be a way to process written information like how we process everything else from sight.

That led me on a quest. I scoured the internet for reading systems, researched everything about how the eyes work, and even experimented with different ways of reading – looking at the top half of words, the bottom half, skipping words, looking at only the sides, and on and on.

One day, I began looking at the spaces between every 3-4 words, and voila, the technique was born! Paying attention to the white space prevents the eyes from narrowing their focus, thus, fixating on individual words. As a result, the eyes can pick up more information, just as when they look at someone's face.

By focusing only on the dots – the spaces between the words – the mind was able to rapidly capture the text. Remember, simply look at the dots in between the words, and move swiftly from one dot to the next.

That's all!

Just as when you look at a tree, a car, or anything else in the environment, the mind picks up the information without you having to think about or work at it. That's what your marvelous eyes and brain are designed to do!

Then, to read faster, the transition from looking at the spaces between every two words to looking at the spaces between every three words. Then every four words. With enough practice, you can advance to looking at only a few spaces per row of text to quickly grasp the information in that row.

Let's try the exercise again with the dots spaced between every three words. Below is the same paragraph as above, but with dots between every three words. As before, bounce your eyes from one dot to the next in quick succession.

However, don't immediately jump to this level. Practice first with a space between every two words. Once comfortable there, move up to glancing at spaces between every three words. Move up to one space every four words only when you are proficient with three. You will eventually reach a level where you can absorb an entire sentence by merely glancing at two spaces, one in the middle left and then the middle right.

Some people advance to such a level that they need to glance only at one space—the one in the middle—to capture the entire line of text. They read by moving down one row to the next, gazing only at the space in the middle of each line.

If you didn't see the magic in this or could not pick up the text the first time, try the exercise again. Remember, look only at the dots between the words in the above paragraph, and move swiftly from one dot to the next. This time, try softening your gaze a bit.

In the beginning, avoid the need to comprehend what you are reading. Simply focus on developing the habit of looking at the spaces and moving from one space to the next. Understanding and comprehension will come naturally since the mind evolved to derive meaning from information the eyes take in. Trust the mind to construct meaning without conscious effort on your part.

It's the natural way the eyes and mind work to process information. Therefore, you need only change the habit from looking at words to looking at the spaces between those words.

Which brings us to the . . .

Practice drill

This drill will train the eyes to shift focus from looking at words to looking at spaces between words. To start, scroll back to the beginning of this chapter and reread it using the technique of Space Reading, which means moving the eyes from one blank space to the next without stopping. Remember not to analyze, evaluate, or try to make meaning. Your only goal right now is to bounce from one space to the next in quick succession.

After going through the chapter once, repeat the drill, but this time, move the eyes between spaces every two words. Make sure to do this throughout the entire chapter. It will go faster this time because you are stopping in fewer spaces. When you finish, begin again with every three words.

Finally, reread the chapter while looking at spaces between every three words.

As you become comfortable, reread this chapter one more time, looking at spaces every four words while also trying to make sense of the words and their meaning. You might need to go slower because now, you are actively involved in making sense of the content.

After completing this step, practice reading while looking at spaces every four words on the materials gathered for the previous drill—articles, reports, and even email and social media posts. Get the eyes accustomed to doing this with big text, small text, text with wide columns, and short columns.

Looking at spaces between words is one technique that directly impacts reading speed and ability. The next chapter will cover the second technique, called chunking. Both methods keep the eyes from fixating on individual words so that you can naturally soak in more information (Please note: Space Reading is trademarked and cannot be reproduced without prior express written permission).

Chunking

Looking at chunks is far better than looking at hunks–Kam Knight

In this chapter, you will learn another deceptively simple trick to boost reading called chunking. Unlike the previous technique of Space Reading, which focused on looking at the spaces in between words, chunking involves looking at the words themselves. However, instead of looking at words one at a time, you glance at groups, or chunks, of words.

Chunking works on the same principle as Space Reading. As you learned, the eyes can process an image or object either in its entirety or in distinct parts. When looking at a distinct part, the eyes instinctively focus on that part to exclude all others. This causes us to miss everything around it.

Consider what happens when a camera takes a picture of a close object. The background becomes blurred. Conversely, when there is no object in close view, the background is clear.

The same principle applies to our eyes. When we look at a word, the eyes' natural tendency is to narrow their field of vision to that one specific word while disregarding the words around it. That leaves us no choice but to read text one word at a time.

Chunking opens our line of sight to capture more words in a single glance. The eyes are not set on a single word of a sentence, but instead, on a block, or chunk, of words in that sentence. You look at a chunk, move to another chunk, then another, and so on.

Let's look at an example. Below is a paragraph very much like the sample paragraph in the previous chapter. This time, the paragraph is separated into chunks with the "/" character. Position your eyes on the first chunk, and look at all the words together as a whole. Then, move the eyes to the next chunk and then the next in rapid sequence.

Even though you / are not looking / at individual words / in this paragraph / your eyes and mind / are still able / to pick up the text. / This happens because / paying attention to / chunks of words / prevents your eyes / from narrowing their focus / on individual words.

As with Space Reading, you were able to capture the text without focusing on individual words. And just as with Space Reading, you increased reading speed simply by changing the way you look at words. You may have thought that you wouldn't be able to read text more than one word at a time, but as you just experienced firsthand, the eyes and mind do, indeed, have the ability to grab a group of words in a single glance.

The key to this technique is not to grab words at random but to grab combinations that form a phrase. If you notice, the previous paragraph is broken into meaningful units: In this paragraph, at individual words and your eyes and mind. These combinations have meaning, and such combinations help the mind pick up chunks as one large, meaning-rich word.

If possible, avoid combinations like:

/ this paragraph your eyes /

/ and mind are still /

/ the text. This happens. /

Such combinations are difficult to understand, and therefore, difficult to process. Consequently, they keep you from reaching your maximum potential. At the same time, there isn't only one correct phrase combination either: different people can select different chunks in any given sentence, which can still be classified as a phrase.

You've now learned two direct techniques to increase reading speed—Space Reading and chunking. Both techniques work on the same principle of softening the eye's gaze and moving over multiple words in a single glance.

Although both work on the same principle, they function independently of one another. That is, they can't necessarily be used together because it is difficult to effectively look at a space and chuck at the same time. When reading, you will either look at spaces or at chunks of words, but not both.

Since the two techniques operate independently, it is best to choose one to develop. Neither is right or wrong, neither is better or worse.

It's really a matter of preference. Personally, I prefer Space Reading because it is easy and natural for me. Though, you may feel that way about chunking.

The best way to determine which technique you prefer is to practice the drills in the two chapters. You might like both, finding that Space Reading works better with some types of material, while chunking works better with others, which is perfectly acceptable. Whichever you prefer, refrain from using both at the same time.

Practice Drill

This drill requires — you guessed it — rereading this chapter using chunking. First, reread the chapter chunking two words at a time. Then read it, chunking three words at a time. Finally, four words at a time. With each pass, focus only on grabbing words in chunks and not on making sense of the words in the chunks.

Once you are comfortable grabbing chunks of four words, the next step is to pick out chunks that form phrases. This step may be challenging, so you may need to slow down considerably, even stopping to analyze whether a particular chunk makes up a phrase, or perhaps, a better combination exists.

Allow yourself to go as slowly as needed. It's what you and your mind need to get a feel for what makes good phrases. This is why these practice drills are important — they provide the breathing room to do that.

With consistent practice, you will find that picking out phrases becomes second nature. You will be able to do it with little effort; it will just happen. Still, you have to start somewhere, and there is no better place than with this drill.

Once you get the hang of picking out phrases, the final part of the drill is to read the chapter while making sense of how the phrases come together to form sentences and paragraphs. As before, take the exercise beyond this chapter and onto the other materials.

As with anything in life, speed reading is about increasing habits that speed you up while decreasing habits that slow you down. So far, this section outlined two habits that speed up reading. Now, let's turn attention to a not-so-effective habit that slows it down.

Subvocalization

Think before you speak. Read before you think–Fran Lebowitz

This section teaches you how to break a habit known as subvocalization, which can double or even triple your reading speed by itself. The act of pronouncing any word that is read is known as subvocalization. When subvocalizing, you either speak the words aloud, hear them spoken in your head, or move your lips to match the pronunciation. Each of these actions is a type of subvocalization.

Subvocalization slows down your reading speed by adding an extra step (or steps) to your reading process. You are hearing and/or saying the term in addition to seeing it.

Speech, on the other hand, is a relatively slow operation. Our minds can't talk as quickly as they can see. This makes reading quicker than we talk difficult. We push the mind to read slower than its capacity by vocalizing words out loud or in our heads. In essence, the mind is required to perform two functions at the same time.

Remember the exercise from the introduction? When asked to notice everything in the immediate environment, did you verbalize what you saw? Probably not. Or, do you verbalize everything you encounter while walking down the street? That's a building, that's a sidewalk, and there's a street sign...I see another building and now another street sign.

Of course not.

Instead, we take in what the eyes capture without adding the additional step of vocalizing.

If you did stop to vocalize it all, imagine how long that would take. You would have to walk significantly slower to ensure you caught everything. It's the same when we vocalize while reading. Our pace is significantly reduced.

And slower reading isn't the only side-effect of subvocalization. When subvocalizing, we increase the chances of getting bored. Most of our inner thoughts are spoken in a monotone, expressionless manner, and subvocalizing is often done in the same manner. In other words, we tend to read in the same unexciting tone that we use when talking to ourselves.

As a result, the text just drones on and on inside our heads, and before we know it, we're tired, uninterested, and perhaps, even starting to daydream. We might assume the material we were reading was causing that boredom, but in reality, the cause was simply the sound of our inner voice!

What's more, pronouncing every syllable of every word slows reading even further. Believe it or not, many readers actually take the time to carefully pronounce every word.

If unsure about whether you subvocalize, try this: while reading the next few paragraphs or pages in this book, notice whether or not your lips move, even slightly, or if you hear yourself say the words out loud. If you do either, you subvocalize. Though don't be too hard on yourself; most people are guilty of this habit.

We either start whispering these sounds in our minds or begin moving our lips so others can't hear us. Most people continue reading this way for the rest of their lives, hearing the little voice in the back of their mind and moving their lips to that voice.

Clearly, at one point, vocalization was a necessary evil. However, once we've learned to read, subvocalization is no longer needed. Since the eyes and brain can read and comprehend all on their own, subvocalizing simply gets in the way of your true potential.

Also, as mentioned, information is received faster from sight than is received from hearing or speaking. Relying on sight alone immediately increases reading speed because you go from glancing at words to directly understanding their meaning without any steps in between. As stated, simply by eliminating subvocalization, you can double or triple reading speed right here and right now.

Removing Subvocalization

As beneficial as it is to silence the inner narrator, though, it's not easy. As you learned, it takes time and effort to break long-lasting habits. Nonetheless, the following suggestions reduce the difficulty.

Close Your Mouth

First and foremost, close your mouth when reading. Talking activates many parts of the body, such as the lips, mouth, tongue, jaw, and throat. Subvocalization does as well but to a lesser degree. Despite being less, it still affects speed.

Keeping the mouth closed disengages these processes, thus preventing you from saying the words out loud or moving your lips to their pronunciation. You'll be surprised how much this single, deliberate action can curb the urge to verbalize.

Read Faster than Speech

Read at a fast enough pace where you simply cannot pronounce words or think about their sounds. Humans speak one word at a time and not three or four.

The more words you grab simultaneously, the more you disrupt the habit of sounding them out. Do this quickly. Move between spaces or chunks so fast that the part of you that needs to sound out or hear the words can't keep up.

Hum

Another option involves humming. Hum a tune, song, or a basic melody. Humming works because it preoccupies the vocal cords so that you can't speak or whisper any words.

Humming also drowns out the voice in your head, along with any distracting noise in the immediate environment. If, for example, you are reading around noisy neighbors or loud machinery, humming can replace those annoying sounds with something more soothing.

As an added benefit, humming can set a rhythm and pace to your reading. To speed up reading, hum faster. If you are reading uncontrollably fast and need a way to slow down, hum slower. Humming is an effective way to control reading speed and pace.

The only drawback to humming is that in a public setting, it might distract or annoy others. In these situations, hum in your head; that is, imagine the sound of the humming. Or hum with your breath, breathing to the sound of the tune or song.

This is a slightly more difficult suggestion to master because it involves engaging in two unrelated activities: reading and humming. They are two activities you've likely never done together, so it may be challenging at first. But if you find humming effective, it's a skill worth developing. And as with any skill, consistent practice makes it second nature.

Music

The last and most popular option to break the subvocalization habit is to listen to music. Play it loud enough so that you can't hear yourself think because if you can't hear yourself think, you won't be able to hear yourself read.

Research shows that music without words or lyrics, such as classical, instrumental, or electronic music, is the best reading option. Lyrics in a song compete with words in a text for the mind's attention. Without lyrics, extraneous words aren't getting in the way.

These are some ways to eliminate subvocalization. They are not difficult to implement but do require shifting habits, which isn't always easy. By sticking to them, you will start reading faster almost immediately.

Practice Drill

Begin by closing your mouth to adjust to reading without moving your lips. This will come naturally to those who already read this way, but it will be a bigger struggle for others than it initially seems. After every few sentences, you may catch yourself unknowingly opening or moving your lips.

Each time you catch yourself subvocalizing, stop and close your mouth before moving forward. To really ingrain this habit, any time the lips part, return to the beginning and start the exercise again.

Once you are accustomed to reading with your mouth closed, advance to reading without hearing or sounding out any words. Use the Space Reading or chunking techniques to move through the words quicker than you can speak them. To create an even larger buffer, try humming.

Don't worry just yet about comprehension but only about moving through the text without engaging the verbal or auditory senses. When you can comfortably space read or chunk without any form of vocalization, read the passages once again, this time for comprehension. Remember to carry the practice to the other materials.

This wraps up Section II on the specific speed reading techniques. Now that you know the techniques let's discuss ways to enhance them, which we cover in the next section.

6. HOW YOU CAN SPEED UP

Before you begin to increase your reading speed, I want to introduce you to a powerful speed-up exercise that will enable you to quickly double your reading speed.

Look at the diagram below that visually outlines this exercise, and then I will say how it works to you.

Minute 1: Comprehension Rate

A----- →B

Minute 2: Double Your Comprehension Rate

B---------- →C

Minute 3: Triple Your Comprehension Rate

C-------------- →D

Minute 4: Comprehension Rate

D---------- →

Your exercise is very simple. It is built around a four-minute exercise that is repeated four times. During the first minute, you will read at your peak comprehension rate.

This means you never read faster than you can comprehend. You will learn some easy-to-use hand motions in this program that will enable you to read at your peak comprehension speed quickly and easily.

During the second minute, you will double your reading speed. This means you will be reading twice as fast as your top comprehension rate.

So what happens? You get confused. So confused that your brain will switch on your visual processor.

It is important to remember that during the second minute, you will not be comprehending information.

During the third minute, you will triple your reading speed. This means you will be reading three times faster than your top comprehension rate, causing you to get very confused.

Again this is a good thing because you want to get confused.

During the fourth minute, you again read at your peak comprehension rate, and something amazing will happen. Your peak comprehension speed will be higher than it was during the first minute.

You repeat this four minute exercise four times in a row for a total of sixteen minutes.

This easy to perform exercise will quickly double your reading speed by tricking your brain into thinking that faster is slower. Actually, this mental magic is related to the game of baseball. Let me explain.

The Baseball Analogy

When you observe a baseball player in the warm-up box, you will find them swinging a bat that has heavyweights on it, or they are swinging several bats at the same time. Why?

Their muscles are getting used to the extra weight. When they go to the plate and swing a single bat, their muscles will use the force needed to swing several bats at once.

As a result, the bat is swung harder, and the ball is hit further. A very similar event happens during your sixteen-minute drill.

Let's take an example: reading the first minute's comprehension rate is 100 words per minute.

This means that during the second minute, you will scan 200 words per minute. You won't be able to understand what you are viewing, but you will be viewing the words at twice your comprehension rate.

During the third minute, you will scan at 300 words per minute, and comprehension will be terrible. During the fourth minute, you go back to your peak comprehension rate, and as if by magic, you will be reading faster.

In this example, your new comprehension rate is 110 words per minute. But it gets better.

During the second drill, your initial comprehension rate is 110 words per minute. During the second minute, you scan at 220 words per minute, and during the third minute, you scan at 330 words per minute.

When you slow down during the fourth minute to read at your comprehension rate, your new reading rate is 125 words per minute.

During the third drill, your initial comprehension rate is 125 words per minute. During the second minute, you scan at 250 words per minute, and during the third minute, you scan at 375 words per minute.

When you slow down during the fourth minute to read at your comprehension rate, your new reading rate is 140 words per minute.

Let's take a closer look at what is happening inside your brain, causing your reading speed to increase.

When you double and triple your reading rate, your brain struggles to comprehend. This causes your brain to switch on your visual area to process text at a much higher speed. Let's use the third drill as an example.

After reading at 375 words per minute, reading 140 words per minute seems much slower to your brain. Your brain perceives 140 words per minute as reading much slower than the 375 words per minute that you just scanned without comprehending.

You feel like you are slowing down, when actually you are speeding up from your starting speed of 125 words per minute.

Each time you perform this four minute exercise, your brain feels like it is slowing down during the fourth minute, when actually it is reading faster than it did during the first minute of your drill.

Do this drill four times in a row, and you will experience a profound increase in your reading speed.

I have created an online video that will make it easy for you to see what I have just taught you about your 16 minute exercise. Since this exercise is highly visual, most people find watching the free video very helpful.

7. KNOW AND UNDERSTAND THYSELF

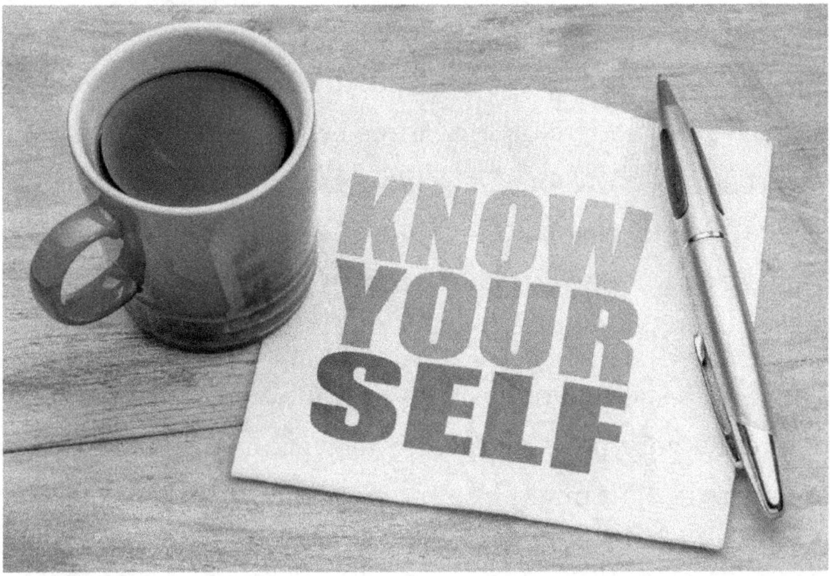
KNOW
YOUR
SELF

The first and foremost step to being better at learning is to know thyself. What that means is to know and understand exactly how you learn and process information the best.

This may come as a surprise to some that people have very different preferences of how they learn. Studies show greater efficacy when exposed to a style or preference that best suits them.

You don't need to take these guidelines as hard evidence, but the simple realization that you can engage information differently should greatly influence the way you learn. You might feel stuck in one way, only to shift to another medium and discover that it works much better for you. You might feel great in one method, shift to another and find that it takes you to the next level.

The point is to have more ammunition in your learning arsenal. If you were in a learning competition with someone else, and they could unleash all their learning potential, because they understood the three best types of information they responded to or knew how to engage themselves in three different ways, you will lose hands down if you have only stuck to one your entire life, even if you're great at it and have it down to a science.

Think of it as if you only spoke French, yet you were forced to read all your news and watch television in Russian. After a few years, you might be pretty good at it, and you might even have methods that work for you, but you'll never be as proficient or efficient as if you could read and watch in French.

That's what not understanding your best learning styles and preferences is like, and that's the risk you run.

Let's get down to it. In this chapter, I only describe two of the main models of learning. There are many more, but these are among the most widespread and prevalent. They further demonstrate that learning and expertise is not a one size fits all approach, and really, it can't be unless you are simply shooting for minimum competency. Remember, while we go through everything presented, try to ask yourself if it sounds like something you might enjoy or hate. Both distinctions are important to make.

The VARK Model of Learning

VARK is an acronym that stands for the four types of learning it splits people into. Neil Fleming developed it. The four types of learning are:

- Visual

- Auditory

- Reading/Writing

- Kinesthetic

If you have a visual style of learning, it means you prefer to see the information so you can actually visualize concepts and how they may or may not connect with others. Try to summarize information in charts, graphs, or even pictures that get the point across in little to no time. At the very least, you can organize notes and information in a way that is visually organized for better absorption. Information that is merely heard or read just doesn't make the same impact and tends to go in one ear and out the other.

Hearing is the best way to process information because it allows you to process that information simultaneously with your own internal train of thought. Reciting information out loud is also helpful because it's an active and conscious act, not like when others do it. To work best, record people as much as possible, including yourself, and think out loud to find your conclusions.

If you have a reading and writing style of learning, you prefer to interact with text and manipulate it. It allows you to process information thoroughly and at your own pace. Reading over notes and summarizing those notes will work best for you, and tactics such as mindmaps also help because they clearly allow you to make connections between concepts. To work best, you should always ask for a written copy, then annotate it yourself with your own notes and thoughts. That way, you can draw your own conclusions and see the evidence right before you.

If you have a kinesthetic learning style, you can't sit still for a lecture or lesson, and you want to experience the topic at hand. You need to try, poke around, and discover for yourself the inner workings of something because simply being told doesn't make much of an impression. You need exercises and problems to solve, trivia to name, and worksheets to fill in. This is the epitome of proactive learning, and it's no surprise that the kinesthetic learning style is effective for many people, whether they realize it or not. It forces participation and active analysis, which is best for memory creation and retention. You work best through seeing demonstrations, then doing them for yourself to pick up anything you might have missed otherwise.

The Seven Learning Styles

The Seven Styles bear quite a few similarities to the VARK model of learning. There is actually overlap in the types of mediums mentioned, and for a good reason: there are five senses, and you can only appeal to them in so many ways. However, where the VARK model seems more conventional and concrete, the seven styles are more geared towards people's innate preferences and

Without further ado, below are the seven styles of learning:

- Visual/Spatial

- Aural

- Verbal

- Solitary

- Social

- Logical

- Physical

Visual learning styles prefer to see pictures, images, movies and generally visualize whatever they are learning directly. Through descriptions of the other learning styles, you will see that visual learner's process information better with their eyes. Seeing something with your eyes is what cements it in your brain. Even if you are reduced to reading or listening, you can replace the words with pictures, use bold colors to highlight areas of importance, and make your notes and outlines easy to comprehend visually. Suppose that you still want to learn the history of Spain. You'd be best suited to studying nautical maps, graphics, charts, seeing movies, and any other visual media that keeps you from having to solely read or listen. Turn your lecture notes into diagrams that hold a lot of information, and make it so you can digest information from a single glance at your page.

Aural learners are also known as musical learners. This is important to distinguish because the VARK method tends to lump them in together with auditory learners. Aural learners don't necessarily prefer listening for better learning; they prefer everything that underlies the appeal of their favorite music. Rhythm, patterns, rhyme, and melody. These are the people that will hum incessantly and make songs for themselves to memorize facts and dates. You might imagine this to be a small minority of learners, but this exists in all of us in reality. It's why we sometimes can't get commercial jingles out of our heads. To better learn Spanish history, you would do your best to work information into existing or new songs and melodies because they come to you easily. The information will be secondary to the music – which is a good thing.

Verbal learners are also known to be linguistic learners, which means they not only prefer words spoken out loud, they prefer to read as well. This type of learner has it easy at first glance because most of the readily available information is in book or lecture form. To learn better, you take what you've heard or read and write it out yourself to strengthen the connections within. To learn Spanish history more effectively, you would take a series of sample test questions, write the answers, and let the insight flow from your pen. If you prefer to use words, you should stick to words and boil any diagrams, graphics, or pictures down to simple descriptions that you can dive into with more detail later. Copious, organized notes that are scribbled over again and again would be normal for this type of learner. You should do your thinking out loud in written form and write questions for yourself to answer later.

Solitary learners represent a point of significant departure from the VARK model, which focused on the types of input that you could receive. The seven learning styles are more holistic definitions that focus on how you best process information. Solitary learners prefer to work alone and process their thoughts by themselves. Everything happens in their own head, and they create their own materials and methods for self-study. They may interact with others, but when it gets down to the wire, they withdraw into a cave with themselves to make connections for themselves. They know what questions to ask themselves and where their knowledge gaps lie. When others explain concepts, it just doesn't have the same impact – they need to think it through step by step for themselves. To learn Spanish history better, the solitary learner would hunker down in a bunker, alone for days with a few textbooks and lectures.

The social learner is predictably the opposite of the solitary learner. They want to seek as wide a set of perspectives as possible to increase their overall understanding. They prefer to see variety, breadth, and diversity of opinion because that will leave no stone unturned. After confirming their questions or beliefs, they can then be confident in what they've learned. To learn Spanish history better, the social learner would engage in a series of role-play or Q&A group study sessions where the information comes out in answers and not through strict reading.

The logical learner prefers to learn through making logical connections and seeing the underlying systems and reasoning. This is the type of person that likes math because there is a single correct method that, if followed, will yield a single correct answer. There is no uncertainty, and almost everything can be explained in some logical manner. You would search for the motivations that create action because understanding the entire context will help with learning the logic. To learn Spanish history better, the logical learner looks at the big picture context of why certain events occurred and the series of events that took place afterward as a consequence. You want to make sense of the world by being able to say, "Oh, that's why that happened. That's the rule," even though it's not always possible.

The physical learner prefers actual physical stimulation for learning. To touch is to experience, and to experience is to know. Using their kinesthetic sense cements information because they are tied to strong feelings and emotions. Sitting stationary in a chair is the worst scenario for this type of learner. They'd much rather get up and interact with others, create materials, interact with demonstrations, role-play, and use their five senses as much as possible. They want to feel, which transmits stronger memories to them. To learn Spanish history better, the physical learner would prefer to explore with their hands as much as possible in museums, folk dance demonstrations, creating models or charts about Spanish history, and have group performances in front of an audience.

This chapter presented two models of learning, with eleven separate ways of processing information. Which ones resonated with you, and which felt like ones you'd ignore as much as possible? Most people are a mixture of multiple methods, so you may take elements from a few of the eleven methods presented. What's important is to know yourself and construct a learning method that best suits your preferences and needs. Only then can you begin to learn like Einstein.

As a final point, there has been increasing scrutiny and criticism about the validity of learning styles. Namely, despite what people deem their styles or preferences to be, it makes no difference as to the overall retention of information.

Is this true? It may very well be. However, learning will always involve sitting still for extended periods; something people can withstand for only varying degrees. Therefore, it might be more helpful and empowering to view each learning style or preference as a tool or trick to make learning more captivating, relatable, or motivating than sitting quietly at a desk by themselves.

8. FASTER AND MORE EFFICIENT READING

Without a doubt, becoming a better reader is tantamount to becoming better at learning.

You might hate reading, or it might be the opposite of your learning style and preferences, but you're not going to be able to avoid it. Most of your initial consumption of information will come through the written word, especially if you are taking your learning into your own hands. What you do with the information after you've consumed it is up to you, but you're still going to start any new learning venture by reading voraciously and consuming as much as possible.

It's the initial gatekeeper that prevents most people from getting into their learning groove. They'll look at a new book or even series of articles and determine it would take them too long to finish, so what's the point? The sense of instant gratification is destroyed when you read slowly or ineffectively. Learning about something new will appear to be a boulder of a task.

That's why becoming a better reader is so important. It's the first step that you'll have to take whenever you want to learn something new.

Being better at reading generally has three parts that I'll cover in more detail: speed, efficiency, and how much is retained.

Reading Faster

For most people that haven't studied speed reading on an individual level, attempting to read too quickly can result in greatly reduced comprehension. This means the faster most people read, the less they understand and can make use of.

This isn't a book that tells you to read as fast as you can. However, you can make a few minor tweaks to your reading pace over time so that what used to take days can now take hours to read and comprehend.

The first trick for speeding up your reading is to reduce the number of sub-vocalizations you use.

Sub-vocalization is actually something you're doing right now. It's when you say and hear the word you're reading in your head. It's a habit that's usually needless, but it's useful when you need to slow down for better understanding. Simply put, we can comprehend and process a word faster than we can say or hear it. Stopping, or at least slowing down, the internal conversation while reading will help you read faster. Hearing sub-vocalizations is only the second and slightly faster stage if reading aloud is the first and slowest.

The second tip for reading quickly is to practice reading several words at once. Reading word for word is slow and inefficient, and it can lead to misunderstandings when you concentrate on the individual word rather than the context or meaning of the text. It's the classic case of being engulfed in the trees and losing sight of the forest as a whole.

Begin by reading two words at the same time. This will take some practice, but once you get the hang of it, you'll find that you don't need to read each word individually. The two words can be thought of as a contraction. When you've mastered two terms at a time, you can progress to three and four words before looking at a ten-word sentence and breaking it down into two five-word sentences. The ultimate aim is to be able to synthesize phrases as easily as individual words. One of the secrets to reading all at once is expanding and dilating your eyes as if you were attempting to use your peripheral vision.

The third tip on speed reading is to improve your visual focus. We constantly lose our place and re-read phrases, and even entire paragraphs, because we get distracted with what's happening elsewhere. This causes you to regress or digress in your reading, which is doubly detrimental to your reading speed. It causes you to have to get back into, "What was this part about, again?"

The simple way to improve your visual focus when reading is to use a placeholder or pointer, such as an index card, pencil, or even your finger. Give your eyes a bulletproof guideline on where to be and where to flow, and they will follow. It will keep you on pace and prevent reading regression from keeping you more immersed in the subject matter.

As I mentioned, this isn't a chapter about speed reading. There are entire books about the subject, and I don't want to do it a disservice. It's a chapter about better and more effective reading, and that's where we will move next.

Efficient Reading

This technique applies mostly to books but also to longer articles and even blog posts.

The underlying idea is most of these books and articles tend to only have one or two big, relevant ideas, tops. Obviously, this differs between topics, but there is generally a good reason most of these sources have a "conclusion" section summarizing all of their findings.

The rest is usually cased studies, anecdotes, speculation, or digressions. This is especially true with non-fiction books, as they can typically be summed up in one page if not for the multitude of case studies, examples, different ways of restating a single concept, and evidence and proof for the assertion. What do we do with this knowledge?

We can use it to read extremely efficiently. Your job with reading is to find those one or two big, shiny ideas and try to cut out the rest of the clutter. This means you don't need to read a book or article from beginning to end. In fact, that would be a mistake and a waste of time.

Note this technique works better for longer pieces since you don't generally need to read shorter pieces more efficiently – they're short!

There are three steps to this technique, and I'll illustrate it with a book example.

The first step is to spend three minutes simply skimming the book's front and back covers, the table of contents, and summary of the book. Think of this as pre-reading the book, and in fact, you just might be able to get everything out of the book in this step. Many books make their big ideas known upfront. If you have time, then you might analyze the introduction or first chapter a bit because the big idea might be there, as well.

The second step is to spend roughly seven minutes skimming the book again but in more depth. This is when you read the two paragraphs of each chapter to find the big ideas of each chapter, and the big pieces of evidence that support the big ideas. If you see a story or anecdote coming, that's a cue to skip ahead because they are usually only for illustration. During this step, you will also make note of sections to read in more detail in the next step.

The third step is to spend twenty minutes reading specific sections of the book in greater detail. You should know the big ideas from the book already, and you are now looking for clarification and what each chapter adds to the big ideas. Review the highlighted portions from the previous step and read them in greater detail. Then, finish this step by synthesizing what you've read and summarize it in five main bullet points, with three bullet points under each – tops.

Some people like to add to the fourth step of reading the first sentence of each paragraph in each chapter, but it is mostly unnecessary to your goal, which is to find the one or two big ideas! At this point, you should have a very clear idea of what's contained in the book, and it only took you thirty minutes. If you lack clarity about a certain concept, then you know exactly where to read it straight from the source.

Retain More

Retaining more of what you read is easier than people think. The problem is that most people see reading as a fairly passive activity. As in, they can just sit back and read, and somehow the information will stick in their memory banks.

That's not quite how it works, and for better memory retention and comprehension, you need to make reading a proactive task. The best type of reading is when you read with a purpose because that will keep you focused and alert as to the information in front of you.

Reading with a purpose also turns you into an asker of questions, which is paramount. After every chapter, page, or even long paragraph, there are a series of questions you can be asking yourself to make sense of the information and make more connections in a participatory manner.

For example, you might ask:

• How does this point relate to the chapter or book in general?

• What did I just learn?

• Why does this matter?

• What are the shortcomings of this?

• What is the counter-argument of this?

• What was necessary for this to occur?

• What is a one-sentence summary of what I just read?

If you are able to actively process these thoughts even occasionally throughout your reading, you will retain far more because the information isn't just a set of facts anymore. They have created a series of connections that you have justification and context on. It's the difference between hearing a bunch of musical notes and hearing an orchestra play together. It creates a bigger impact on your memory because they now have meaning to you through the analyzing questions.

One of the best ways to synthesize and retain information better is to try to predict what happens next or what happens as a consequence of what you've just read. When you can pull enough information together to make an informed guess, it requires a level of thought and understanding that goes far beyond passive reading.

For example, imagine the kind of thought process you would need if you were to do this with a movie. You would need to think about the hints that were shown, the motivations and thought processes of the characters, what might typically happen in a similar movie, and why the previous scene influenced you. You could probably list all of these things if asked about the movie prediction, which shows that you are engaged and invested. We can do similar things when we learn. You don't have to make a correct or even good prediction, and the important part is to think about what you've seen, try to create patterns, and analyze them.

Finally, to retain more when you read, start from the end. Don't read backward, but read and review differently from how you initially consumed the information. For a book, start from the final points of the last chapter and work your way to the introduction. For an article or study, work your way from the conclusion back to the introduction. What's the point of this?

When you continually read something in the same order, you're creating tread marks in the mud. In other words, you are solidifying information, but only in that specific order and context. You might only retain and remember something if you read or remember what was immediately before or after it.

It's similar to listening to a song playlist in the same order, over and over. Eventually, it all melds into one long song, and you can remember and predict the next song based on the current song. But, out of that order and context, you might not be able to remember or think of it.

9. HOW TO CRAM

However, despite the many opinions advocating spaced repetition or early learning, many of us still do not.

That's for a good reason. We get busy with other things and can't break our stride to review something even for five minutes. We have many other subjects to learn and study. We just feel lazy and tired at the end of a long day. These are all legitimate excuses.

We know this isn't the most effective way to learn, but unfortunately, it's what we're stuck with sometimes. There's a saving grace – recall that most effective learning targets long-term memory. That's the main goal of spaced repetition: making the leap from short-term memory to long-term memory, where you no longer have to rehearse or practice it to remember it. You can simply recall it with a bit of thought, and it's in your brain for an indefinite time.

To cram for a test, exam, or another type of evaluation, we don't need material to make it to our long-term memory. We just need it to make it slightly past our working memory and be partially encoded into our long-term memory. We don't need to be able to recall anything the day after, so it's like we only need something to stick to for a few hours.

This chapter optimizes for learning as much as possible in as little time as possible while also ensuring that you can retain it. It's a difficult task, but if you're going to pull an all-nighter, you might as well do it in the right way.

Chunking

I discussed chunking briefly in the previous chapter, but it's more appropriate to discuss it in detail here. Chunking is the act of turning five pieces of information into one piece of information for the sake of memorization.

For example, which is easier to memorize: 3 3 5 9 1 0 or 33 59 10? That's how chunking works. You do it every time you try to keep an account or telephone number in your memory before you use it. You simply combine information on a conceptual or semantic level such that your memory has to hold fewer objects.

Recall that our short-term memories can only hold seven items on the top range. Chunking gets around this because where there were once six numbers to remember, now there are three. That's a type of chunking that is called grouping. You create something to memorize from seemingly unrelated and random pieces of information

If you have a list of things to purchase, you can create a mnemonic device, like mentioned previously, where the first letter of each item forms a new word. If you want to buy pears, apples, bananas, and underwear, that forms the word PABU, which is easier to remember or write down.

For the same list of things to purchase, you can also just push the words together. If you want pears, apples, bananas, and underwear, you could remember the word "pe-ap-ba-un," representing all of the information on the list. You're substituting four pieces of information for one.

Another example is to visualize a scene or environment where all the elements work together. See a picture mentally of a setting that contains all of the items mentioned above, and keep in mind there are four of them total. Where might you see three pieces of fruit and a pair of underwear? Perhaps a hoarder's kitchen table or an obscene grocery store. The more vivid the setting, the more memorable it will be.

In each of these cases, you're creating something new or referring to something already in your memory that reminds you of multiple pieces of information. Make a connection and create something meaningful, which is easier to remember. This is the reason raw data and information rarely ever make it to long-term memory. The moment you can see a pattern form, it is easier to remember.

Pomodoro Technique

The Pomodoro Technique is a focus technique that promotes undistracted work and planned breaks. It's straightforward. You look at your study time in thirty-minute blocks. You will focus, turn off your phone, and ignore all distractions for twenty-five minutes, and then take a planned break for only five minutes to give your brain a break to not run at full capacity. This is one block, and immediately after, you dive into another thirty-minute block.

Most practitioners of the Pomodoro Technique make it their goal to complete eight thirty-minute blocks, but you might find that difficult if you're new to the concept. My recommendation is to aim for three blocks at first and see how you feel at that point.

The greater purpose of the Pomodoro Technique is to avoid multitasking and wasting mental capital switching between tasks and backtracking while you try to find where you were. This frequently will result in one step forward and one step backward, and after a couple of hours, you might find that you've only made minimal progress across all your tasks. Complete attention and focus for twenty-five minutes, no small amount of time, will allow you to build momentum and really make way through your information.

What's more, you'll likely overshoot twenty-five minutes, in which case, you should take a ten-minute break after fifty minutes.

The Pomodoro Technique often makes you aware of the importance of taking breaks and avoiding distractions. Normally, we can't maintain complete concentration all of the time. You can't run indefinitely without tiring out; finally, you'll need to take a rest. That's when you realize you need to take a break. And when you're cramming, it's a normal part of the memorization and learning method.

Continually Summarize

Remember, there's limited time and limited space in your memory banks when you're cramming, so you need to consume and memorize as little information as possible that will impart as much meaning as possible.

The goal is to give meaning and association to smaller pieces of information. Essentially, you want to be able to cram a paragraph's worth of information and recall it into a single sentence. The way to do this is to re-write and re-summarize your notes into shorter and shorter versions until they can ideally all fit onto a single piece of paper (or even an index card, depending on the context). Ideally, you also write this all by hand because you are forced to be economical with your words when writing by hand.

Let's say you start with ten pages of notes, which you first summarize and condense into three pages. This will force you to analyze what's important and filter all the clutter in your subject matter. You'll also begin memorizing on a deeper level when you review your material with this type of goal. Then, you summarize the three pages into one page. The act of combing through your material and thinking, "Is this important and does this contribute to the overall point?" is just as important as the actual act of writing out the new summary version.

Finally, you might summarize your single page so it fits onto an index card, which will further force you to condense, filter, and analyze the important parts. By this point, you've essentially written your notes three additional times, but in a way that is friendly to your limited memory banks at the moment. What's more, it's not like you will only remember what is only on the index card. Each sentence and bullet point will have so much more meaning and information behind it because you've filtered it three times and thought about it deeply.

You're working with limited space, and continually summarizing your material is going to make the most of it.

Make Connections

Raw information on the page isn't going to make it to your memory very easily. What you must do is give meaning to it, make it relate to the information you already know, and simply make it memory-worthy.

First, make sure you understand your material. When you comprehend something, it will be easier to cram into your brain than something that is a puzzle to you.

Second, actively seek to make as many connections to existing knowledge as possible by continually asking, "It's like X, except Y..." It doesn't matter if it's not particularly related. Just make a connection as to how they might relate. It's this deeper analysis that hardcodes information, not the actual analogy, metaphor, or comparison. Additional questions to ask to make connections to existing information are, "It's the opposite of X..." and "This has the following three elements in common with X..."

Third, reason out loud to yourself. This is where you use phrases such as, "So this X happened because Y..." and "Z only occurred because X..." You're basically narrating how everything fits together. Understanding context and logical flow will help your memorization.

Use Space

You might not be able to do true spaced repetition if you are cramming at the last minute, but you can emulate it in a small way. Instead of studying subject X for three hours only at night, seek to study it one hour every three times a day, with a few hours between each exposure.

Recall that memories need time to be encoded and stick in the brain. You are doing the best imitation of spaced repetition you can with what you have available. To get the most out of your limited studying time, study something as soon as you wake up, review it at noon, at 4:00 p.m., then 9:00 p.m. – or similar. The point is to review throughout the day and get as much repetition as possible.

During your repetition, make sure to study your notes out of order to see them in different contexts, encode better, and use active recall versus passive reading.

Finally, make sure that you're reciting and rehearsing new information until the last minute before your test. Your short-term memory can hold seven items on its best day, so you might just save yourself with a piece of information that was never going to fit into your long-term memory. It's like you're juggling. You inevitably drop everything, but it could just so happen that you're juggling something you can use.

10. YOUR NEW READING EXPERIENCE

There certainly does seem to be an endless flow of words today. Unlike a short time ago, when our access to words was limited to the space available on our bookshelves or to the amount of time we could spend in our local library, today we have an infinite amount of reading material available literally. It's easier than ever to access, and it's there for us twenty-four hours a day. Our biggest challenges now are deciding what to read and how to get through it all.

Today there really is only one limit to the information available, and that limit is us. Our reading speed is the only limit to the many things we can know and the many stories we can experience.

Superior reading skills can give us greater access to this expanding cornucopia of information, and access to this information can have a powerful effect on our lives. It can make our lives easier, happier, and even safer and healthier — which might even mean longer! Plus, this greater access to information will also make our lives more interesting and make us more interesting.

In addition to acquiring information, improved reading skills can even physically enhance our brains. Reading skills also strengthen our brains by boosting memory, focus, concentration, and analytical thinking.

But wait, there's more! Conceptualizing information and really paying attention to its meaning will increase your awareness of life. Instead of having a superficial awareness of the things you see, hear, and read — conceptual thinking will make you more aware of the deeper reality of what things actually mean.

Your Reading Upgrade

Conceptualizing ideas instead of listening to sounds is learning to experience reading in a new way. This is a major upgrade to those very old reading lessons from your childhood.

- The Unread Masses

Unfortunately, poor readers aren't lonely; they have many more companies than good readers have. There are sadly more and more people who, for one reason or another, have either not progressed in their reading skills after childhood or have even regressed through a lack of practice. Sure, they may read their text messages and tweets, and maybe even headlines and picture captions, but a large number of people shy away from anything more demanding than the TV Guide, and they restrict the selection of what they read to material with plenty of pictures. When there is more information than ever easily available to us, we are turning into a readerless society.

- Time

How much time does it take to read a book? Remember that the average adult reads two hundred words per minute. Assume this average person wants to read a three hundred pages long and has approximately four hundred words per page. This book would then have a total of one hundred twenty thousand words. This book would take ten hours to read (120,000 / 200 = 600 minutes or 10 hours). However, at four hundred words per minute, this book would only take half that time — five hours.

So how long would it take this average person to learn to increase his reading speed from reading two hundred words per minute to four hundred? Four hundred words per minute is not actually a very difficult speed to reach. If it took a total of five hours of practice to learn this speed increase, then those five hours would be saved back after reading only one book. But a reading speed increase is a gift that keeps on giving because the faster a person reads, the more books they will want to read, and therefore, the more time they will get back.

Besides this time rebate, what about the benefits side of the equation? The major benefit, of course, is improved comprehension. This means getting more out of your reading. When someone asks, "What is that book about?" you can actually tell him.

But there are even more benefits to gain from improved reading skills.

- Power

The mental exercise of reading develops a more powerful mind. The act of reading is one of the most sophisticated mental achievements of the human mind. The mental exercise this involves strengthens your intelligence, sharpens your analytical skills, and improves your ability to separate reality from fiction.

Even more, power can be developed by extending your reading to your right brain. One way is by improving the power of your memory. By conceptualizing phrases, you concentrate on more complex ideas, making your reading more memorable and storing information more efficiently. You are not just reading new information but conceptualizing it and associating it with previous information. Each of these complex memories creates even more association points for future memories to attach to.

- Success

Reading — combined with the ability to understand, recall, and make use of the material you have read — also plays a major role in achieving success in life.

Faster reading and better comprehension have powerful impacts, whether it's better informed in your job, or having a better understanding of your studies, or simply by being a more well-rounded and informed conversationalist.

Good reading skills produce many advantages. It's no exaggeration to say that in this modern interconnected and competitive world, the ability to read, comprehend, and better organize information into useful knowledge could be considered equivalent to a survival skill and a prerequisite to the most success.

- Uniqueness

By concentrating on concepts, you will remember the facts and the real meaning behind what you read as well. You can't remember every detail you read, but you can remember the meaning. Your own personal meaning is created by the selection and significance of attributes you connect to information — these selections being based primarily on your previous knowledge and interests.

These conceptual connections are what make each of us unique. Each person has his own informational combinations, and these combinations and intersections of information create each person's uniqueness, enabling each person to see information in unique ways with unique perspectives.

This is true of all kinds of reading. No matter what you read, all reading changes you. In a lot of ways, we are what we read. We are the sum of these experiences, and many of our experiences come to us vicariously through reading, from anywhere and from anywhen.

- Innovation

It's the conceptual connections of information that create the real power of human intelligence. The information itself is cheap—the whole world of information is only a Google search away. The real power of human intelligence is not in the collection of information but information connections. At these unique intersections, ideas build upon each other to produce new, relevant, and valuable ideas. These unique combinations are the real mother of innovation.

Read for Enjoyment

Many people who say they don't have time to read will also say they don't have time to learn to read faster, but this seems like a contradiction since reading faster could save them time.

When you are facing a contradiction, check your premises; you will usually find that one of them is wrong. I believe the mistaken premise here the belief that those people want to read in the first place.

I suspect the real truth is that most people don't want to read simply because it's not enjoyable for them. I hope one benefit of conceptual reading is to make reading more enjoyable. I have found that by improving my own reading, I've developed what feels almost like a reading addiction.

So why not deemphasize the collection of raw data and instead concentrate on developing intelligence by fostering your reasoning ability and creativity — which are all enhanced through the connectedness of information and conceptual reading of ideas?

Realistic Expectations

Of course, every skill takes practice, but at least this is a practice that works. This is not practicing some so-called secret speed-reading tricks — like the ones you find in every other book. This is practicing seeing the ideas behind the words by concentrating on the larger blocks of information.

But let's be realistic—there are many very unbelievable claims being made in the speed reading industry. You're probably suspicious of many of them, or you at least suspect they might be too good to be true.

Instead of filling your head with nonsense, I want to give you something that will truly be of value to you. Forget all the exercises that focus on eye movement. Instead, focus on thinking conceptually about what you are reading by employing the right side of your brain to see the big picture, the whole idea of what you read.

With the explosion of information available through e-readers and the internet, we are likely witnessing a fundamental transformation of the world. In fact, we are probably at the beginning of unprecedented information and knowledge revolution—a quantum leap in the development of human intelligence and potential. The driver of this change is the worldwide connectedness and collaboration that has suddenly been made available through the internet.

All of this change, however, depends on reading. A rocket ship is about to take off, headed for the future, but only those with excellent reading skills will be aboard.

11.   TEXTING THE BRAIN

Thinking about how you're reading while reading can seem counterproductive because the extra effort required would probably distract you from your comprehension. You can really only think of one thing at a time, so thinking about what your brain is doing would interfere with thinking about what you are reading.

But an overall concept of how the brain reads will help you to practice more effectively. An overview of what your brain is doing and what you are trying to change will help you stay on the right track and stay focused on the techniques that will get your right brain more involved.

It's unnecessary to stay consciously aware of this process while you read, but removing some of the mystery may leave you with a general lay of the land to make your progress more straightforward by giving you an idea of what you're trying to change.

Mechanics

The text is a sending device in basic terms, and the reader's mind is a receiving device. Just like a text message sent from one smartphone to another, printed words are sent from the page to your brain. In both cases, a signal is being sent, received, and then decoded.

How does the brain actually accomplish this task? How can you know someone's thoughts simply by looking at squiggles on a page? It seems like some kind of magic that these printed marks are speaking to your brain. How is this possible? Text enters the eyes like any other image, but how do images of text turn into thoughts? Where and how does real reading take place?

This is not a course on neurolinguistics — and anyone who is an expert in the field is invited to clarify any essential discrepancies — but basic concepts will still be useful, so here are a few simple glimpses under the hood to help conceptualize what is involved.

Like all mental tasks, reading uses a network of modules and systems, each relying on its own network of neurons. Many areas of the brain work together simultaneously, and while the complete process is not entirely understood yet, a general awareness of how reading is accomplished can give you a deeper respect for the amazing complexity involved, as well as an appreciation of how and why reading with the right brain boosts your reading effectiveness.

One network of neurons, which many people may not think of as an actual part of the brain, is the eye. Reading starts with light entering the eye. And even though the whole eye is filled with light, only the fovea — a portion of the retina which occupies about fifteen degrees of the visual field — is used for reading.

Signals from the fovea are transferred to the occipital lobe at the back of the brain, where the light signals are recognized as shapes. From this point on, these shapes are converted into words in a step-by-step process along a path through the left side of the brain.

The recognized shapes are passed from the occipital lobe to the visual recognition area, where shapes are recognized as letters and then passed further to Wernicke's area. This is the area that understands both written or spoken language. This area recognizes the groups of letters as words. From here, the information branches off in several more directions.

The words are sent farther forward to the hearing area in the auditory cortex, where they can be subvocalized, plus along a separate path to Broca's area, where speech production is controlled for saying words aloud.

At the same time, the words are also sent down into the center of the brain to the amygdala, where the emotional content is determined. It may not seem like emotions would affect reading, but memories are more likely to stick if they are combined with emotion. This is one reason that having an interest in a subject makes it easier to remember; being interested in something activates the powerful emotion of pleasure.

But there's much more to reading than just recognizing words. Real meaning only comes from the way the words are combined, and in that one fact lies the real secret to reading faster...

Think Fast

Quick! Memorize the following letters:

U P S I R S F B I J F K N A S A N A T O

Not done yet? Fine. Give up then, because it really will take too long.

But let's make it easier by grouping the same string of letters like this:

UPSI RSFB IJF KNA SAN ATO

Easy, right? Just six little "words" to remember. Nope. Easier, but still too hard and still takes too much time.

Well, what if we group the letters like this:

UPS IRS FBI JFK NASA NATO

Wow, what a difference! The letters still make up six words, but these words are so much easier to remember. They're made up of the same letters, in the same order, and in the same number of "words," but only the grouping is different. Now they're grouped into phrases, with each phrase representing a meaningful chunk of information.

This is the key to moving more information through your brain faster: parceling the information into larger meaningful packages. Reading and remembering take a lot of thinking, and this thinking takes time. You can't really make those neurons fire any faster than they are capable; they still have physical limits as smart as they are.

I don't mean that neurons are slow, but it just takes a lot of firing on their part to accomplish the work they have to do as they sort and store information. When they're resting, neurons fire about twenty-five times per second. When they're active, that speed increases to around four hundred times per second. And when they're concentrating really hard on something, they max out at about one thousand firings per second. So yes, you can think faster, but there is still a maximum speed limit.

There are other limits, too. Besides processing speed, our conscious minds can only hold about seven pieces of information at a time, and at normal reading speeds, these pieces only have about half a second before the next piece comes through.

But fortunately, there is a clever way to bypass both of these limitations. In fact, this solution is a special talent that, compared to all other creatures, puts humans at the head of the pack in the thinking department. Although humans aren't particularly exceptional at physical abilities, such as strength, speed, eyesight, smell, or hearing, they do excel at consciousness. The uniquely powerful human consciousness gives rise to an amazing ability to handle novel and complex information, allowing humans to invent new solutions to problems and make accurate predictions.

This consciousness is not located throughout the whole brain but resides primarily in the prefrontal cortex. This is where you pay attention. This is where the real "you" lives.

This prefrontal cortex is the erasable whiteboard of the brain; here, information is scribbled temporarily while the consciousness decides what to do with it. Information constantly and rapidly flows into this area from the senses and is quickly organized, filtered, and chunked together into larger ideas. And it has to accomplish all this even though it only has room to hold about seven pieces of information at a time.

But the conscious mind uses a clever trick to keep up with all this information. Although it is limited to handling only about seven items at a time, each of these items can be immensely complex. Each of these seven items can be piled high with information, similar to the way we pile food on our plates at an all-you-can-eat buffet. Chunking of information into larger, more complex ideas makes the most of each conceptual idea before it is sent on to memory.

The key to this process of filtering and combining information uses the brain's fascination with patterns and hidden structures. These patterns allow ideas and concepts to be assembled into massively complex pyramids of information where each thought is attached to many layers of underlying meaning and associations.

This hunger for patterns is unstoppable. We can't help seeing patterns in everything. The result is more than just faster thinking, but also richer life experiences. By filtering and combining information into larger patterns, we create the complex context of our consciousness. We don't just see, learn, and remember information—we understand it conceptually. To conceptualize information is to become truly aware of it and what it means to us.

The process of chunking information into conceptual patterns is not just a neat trick for thinking and reading faster—the more we chunk information into concepts, the more truly conscious we become.

Reading Evolution

So just like language, our minds are just what we ended up with. Our brains weren't designed with reading in mind. Our early hominid ancestors needed to know things like where food and resources were, the route home, and which plants were edible or poisonous.

They had to be very good at visual imagery to recognize these types of things, but they didn't have to remember things like lists of facts or names, dates, and numbers. They also didn't need to spend much time thinking about abstract ideas — the kinds with no visual associations.

In essence, we are still reading with prehistoric brains, yet somehow there are fixed circuitries of the human brain that seem perfectly attuned to recognizing the printed word.

In other words, reading looks to be a patch onto an existing, more primitive brain. But even though this reassignment of brain areas is a makeshift adaptation, our reading skills have continued on a constant path of improvement and sophistication. They have progressed from recognizing cave pictures to rapidly consuming vast amounts of data from a continuous flow of complex information.

This has been an incredible mental restructuring. A caveman has learned to read. If the brain developed this amazing skill in such a short time, then once again, it makes one wonder how we could imagine that our current reading skill is the "finished" product.

12. PHOTOREADING

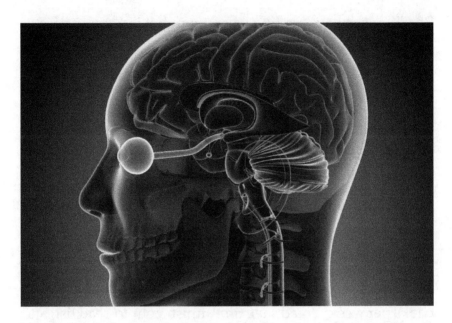

You've already heard of speed reading, but photoreading is something entirely different. Yes, you still read very quickly, but you read at least 25,000 words per minute with this technique. You're not alone if you find that sounds unlikely. However, some argue that the technique is successful. Although scientific evidence in either direction is limited, you can make your own decision based on what we know so far.

What Is the Difference Between Photoreading and Speed Reading?

Speed reading aims to increase your reading speed by two to three times your normal pace. This increases the rate to about 600 wpm for most people (words per minute). This should also allow you to read multiple pages per minute.

Reading is always reading, even though it is done at a faster rate. You simply learn a new way to read, which often entails being shown a single word or sentence at a time to prevent distractions and additional eye movements.

Photoreading, on the other hand, is not a form of reading. It's all about subconsciously photographing each page of a book to be stored and accessed later. You read a new page every second instead of a few pages per minute. Using this approach, you should be able to read a book during your lunch break at work.

Consider the benefits of being able to read hundreds of books per week. You'd save time, finish your to-read list, and learn so much more. Exam preparation will be a breeze. Is photoreading, however, a real possibility?

What Is the Process of Photoreading?

Before delving into whether or not this approach works, it's important to understand how the mechanism works. Scheele is the one who came up with this strategy. To make it work, you must be in the proper mental condition, also known as the whole state or using the whole mind.

The procedure consists of five major steps:

1) Make a straightforward goal for what you're reading and why you're reading it.
2) To construct a mental structure, preview the material using a special technique.
3) Photoreading is a method of "reading" in which you mentally photograph the pages while you read.
4) Use the post-view process to investigate topics you'd like to learn more about.
5) Activate what you've photographed to improve your understanding of a topic.

Obviously, the method is more complicated than that, but that's a general idea. Each phase necessitates advanced techniques, which can be learned in schools, through books, or a self-paced program.

Beginners will reduce their reading time by up to 70%. Over time, you will be able to learn to use photoreading more effectively.

Proof Is Limited

There are two major studies on photoreading, one in favor of the method and one strongly opposed to it. Both are very biased.

First, let's look at the good research. The Learning Strategies course claims a 96 percent success rate for students who are willing to work hard. It also claims to be a synthesis of university-proven reading strategies rolled into a single, highly successful method.

Although there are numerous testimonials available, some well-known writers have spoken out in support of the method. Dr. Ken Blanchard, the author of One Minute Manager, claims that the technique allows him to learn quickly to remain updated on leadership strategies and trends. And he's only one of many people who've increased their reading speeds by using the device.

Then there's the often-cited negative research, which claims that not only does photoreading take longer, but it also reduces reading comprehension. NASA conducted a report to determine if the technique succeeded. The issue is that there were only two participants, one of whom was the individual conducting the research.

Dr. Danielle McNamara, on the other hand, took a photoreading course with another participant. The findings were underwhelming. In fact, when compared to normal reading, output on reading comprehension tests decreased. Furthermore, the whole process seemed to take as long, if not longer, than usual reading speeds. As a result, McNamara concluded that the system is ineffective.

Scheele has since spoken with McNamara about the study's drawbacks, such as the relatively small number of participants. Learning Strategies has since issued a rebuttal, stating why the study is incorrect.

Issues with Reading Faster

Experts also discovered that there is rarely a shortcut in research on speed reading. Skimming is the most powerful strategy, and it works better when you're already familiar with a subject and knows what you're looking for. This helps you to skip through the filler and get right to the good stuff.

The common consensus is that the quicker you attempt to read something, the less understanding you will have. Simply practicing reading skills will teach the brain to identify word and sentence patterns for quicker comprehension.

Though photoreading is special, you must also consume a large amount of information in a short time. As a consequence, comprehension rates may be lower.

Is Photoreading a Real Thing?

Perhaps. Some say that it works for them. However, you must be able to practice the technique and keep your mind calm and free. Consider it a meditative reading state, which may or may not be possible for all.

13. PEGGING INFORMATION

Using the power of our associative mind, we will learn two "peg" methods of memory. The "shape peg" method was developed in 1651 by Henry Herdson, who linked numbers to objects shaped like digits. The "rhyming peg" method was introduced two centuries later by John Sambrook in 1879.

These methods are very simple and effective. They will provide you with a system that can help you remember 40 or more bits of information in a short space of time. You can even access the information in random order and by number.

Rhyming Pegs

The pegs in the rhyming pegs system work similarly to clothes pegs or clothespins in that they hold knowledge floating around in your head. For the pegs to function, they must become part of your long-term memory.

Remember that your long-term memory is still needed to help your short-term memory. You connect new knowledge with long-term "memory pegs" in your mind using this approach. The pegs even serve as filing cabinets for your new ideas.

The technique is straightforward: it creates memory pegs from words that rhyme with numbers. As mental scripts, we'll use the following rhyming words:

The word "one" rhymes with "bun."

Two–shoe

Three–tree

Four–door

Five–hive

Six–sticks

Seven–heave

Eight–gate

Nine–vine

Ten–hen

Each of these pegs can become compartments to store new information. You link the peg (using the SEE principle) to the words that you want to remember.

The "10 emotions of power" are mentioned in Tony Robbins' life-changing book Awaken the Giant Inside. I'd like you to use this new device to help you remember these feelings. Consider them regularly because professional growth will only happen if you know what you need to do.

The 10 emotions of power are:

1)Love and warmth

2)Appreciation and gratitude

3)Curiosity

4)Excitement and passion

5)Determination

6)Flexibility

7)Confidence

8)Cheerfulness

9)Vitality

10)Contribution

Remember to make the images illogical. See the information in your mind for a few seconds.

One–bun: Imagine a warm, heart-shaped bun, or imagine that thousands of warm hearts fly out of a bun. Since a heart is a symbol of love, you will remember that one is love and warmth if you really visualize it.

Two-shoe: Imagine that a preacher is grating a shoe with a cheese grater. The word preacher can remind you of appreciation, and grater, gratitude.

Three-tree: Imagine a cat in a tree, but don't make it logical. Imagine perhaps that the branches look like cats, cats hang off the branches, or cats are growing out of the tree. Curiosity killed the cat. So, three is curiosity.

Then you squeeze passion fruit on the exciting door. Four is excitement and passion.

Five-hive: Imagine determined bees trying to break open a beehive. The bees are a "determined nation." Determination is five.

Six-sticks: Imagine bending a stick into a spiral like a pig's tail; really feel how flexible the stick can be. Six is flexibility.

Eight-gate: See a smiley-face-shaped gate. You cheerfully open the cheerful gate. Eight is cheerfulness.

Ten-hen: Imagine a hen giving you presents. She is a "contributing hen." Ten is contribution.

Practice feeling these emotions because you become good at what you practice. Tony Robbins says, "You are the source of all your emotions; you are the one who creates them. Plant these emotions daily, and watch your whole life grow with vitality that you've never dreamed of before."

The rhyming peg method can be extended by finding additional words that rhyme with the number, e.g.: one —

bun, gun, sun. With this method, you can easily create a peg system to store up to 30 bits of new information.

Shape Pegs

The shape mechanism, the second peg process, transforms numbers into concrete shapes. It works in the same way as the rhyming peg process, except the pegs are in the form of the number this time. Since you already learned the theory in the rhyme list, we won't do an exercise with this scheme. The shape approach simply adds another alternative to the mix.

Use this list to help you remember 10 new facts on your own. Play around with it and have some fun. Here's the rundown:

The Peg System in Action

You can make new peg lists from any list that already exists in your long-term memory. You can make up words and images for each letter of the alphabet (for example, apple, bucket, cat, dolphin), the months of the year, subway stops on your way to work, or any other list you can remember in order. Enjoy experimenting with this approach and coming up with new ways to develop it.

The method you're about to learn is the most amazing tool you'll ever encounter. It will assist you in ways you could never have imagined. It's so easy, and it's been around for 2,500 years, but few people have taken advantage of it. You can use this device to recall enormous amounts of knowledge. It takes some getting used to, but once you do, you'll never go back.

This approach is the most powerful of all the memory systems, in my opinion. It's as easy to use as remembering a path. It may appear to be far too easy to be useful, but it does so because it does not overpower you.

This approach follows the same steps as the car and body lists, but instead of using cars and bodies to store details, we'll use places or markers in a spot, on a journey, or a path.

The following is how it works:

1) Visualize an ordered place in your head, such as a house layout, a shopping center, or the path you take to get to the mall.

2) As we did with the body and car lists, create markers or places in this position or along the way. Make an easy-to-follow series.

3) Make a simple picture of the details you want to recall using the SEE principles.

4) Mark one of the designated locations for each thing you're trying to recall.

In a nutshell, it's as simple as creating a mental location or route to store the information. This system makes recalling vast quantities of data as simple as recalling a trip to the store. You're employing the LTM + STM = MTM formula once more.

The Traveling Method

Let me show you how to use this "journey process" with a simple exercise. We'll remember 12 important concepts from one of John C. Maxwell's books. I like his books because they are often very well organized, making it easier to remember the details. He starts by making a list of the topics he'll discuss, then goes into greater detail about each one.

You can memorize his lists and laws using the programs, and you can become a leadership expert. When data is stored in a memorable matrix, it aids long-term storage and retrieval by attracting more data to it. It's also much easier to use once you have it in your brain because what good is learning if you can't remember it?

In his book Today Matters, Maxwell shares 12 keys that you can focus on each day to be more successful and fulfilled in your life. He calls these keys the "daily dozen" because, as he says, "You will never change your life until you change something you do daily."

Here are the keys:

1)Attitude

2)Priorities

3)Health

4)Family

5)Thinking

6)Commitment

7)Finances

8)Faith

9)Relationships

10)Generosity

11)Values

12)Growth

The majority of people will attempt to memorize the list of details by repeating it over and over. Unfortunately, rote learning and frequent repetition can be tedious and lead to a dislike of learning.

However, the more information you can encode into your brain, the more successful your learning will be. By concentrating your attention and linking each thought to a spot, the journey approach will help you find the "fun" in FrUstratioN. Let's do a little workout together.

To demonstrate how this device functions, I'm going to use four rooms in my home. In my view, the rooms are compartments where I can store new information. Allow me to lead you around the house, and we'll keep track of it.

Check to see if the markers are in a logical order. Then double-check if you have clear storage compartments. The markers should be close together but well spaced out so that each thing you want to recall is saved in its mental register.

Here is a mental map of four rooms in my house and 12 places that we will use:

Room 1 Kitchen: 1-dishwasher, 2-fridge, 3-stove

Room 2 TV room: 4-chairs, 5-TV, 6-exercise bike

Room 3 Bedroom: 7-mirror, 8-closet, 9-bed

Room 4 Bathroom: 10-bath, 11-shower, 12-toilet

If I gave you a box with 12 objects in it, would you be able to place those objects on the furniture in my house? Of course, you would! So all we do is turn the information into something tangible, like an object, and then place it in the room.

Let's start in the kitchen. The first word is attitude. Imagine someone with a really bad attitude jumping into your dishwasher. Clean up his attitude in the machine. SEE it!

Next, imagine writing all of your priorities on the refrigerator door. Use a permanent marker and think about how your priorities are permanently stored on the fridge door.

Imagine a healthy bodybuilder making applesauce on the stove. The apples are a reminder for health.

So what was in the dishwasher? On the fridge? At the stove?

Now let's move to the TV room. The first place in there is the chairs. Imagine your whole family is jumping up and down on the chairs. The more illogical the image, the better it will stick.

Television is in second place. Consider a thought bubble emerging from the television, a thinking machine that also affects our thinking.

Imagine combing (reminds you of the first few letters of commitment) the exercise bike, which is the last place in the building. It is also a willingness to ride the bike regularly.

The mirror is the first thing I see when I walk into my home. Consider money flinging from the mirror. Your financial situation reflects your efficiency.

Place whatever symbolizes confidence for you inside the closet. Every shelf or hanger should be adorned with confidence.

Relationships are the next term we'd like to add to our memory quest, and it's on the bed. You can take your photo here once more.

The bathroom is the final room. Imagine a genie coming out of the bath and granting your wishes. The genie's kindness reminds us to be kind.

Assume the tub is made of gold or that when you turn on the faucet, gold pours out. Gold has a high monetary value and is a symbol of wealth.

Finally, we imagine a tree growing out of the toilet to provide growth.

Try to figure out what word was associated with each location.

It was as easy as walking around my house to learn the 12 keys in Maxwell's book Today Matters. After a few passes through this page, you'll have a good idea of the regular dozen. If you have properly linked the sentences, you will remember them all.

You will get even better results with this method if you use your own environment because you are more aware of the order of the places. Review the list backward, and you will notice that it will all still be there. Doing this makes the images even clearer for your memory.

This is your first memory route or journey, and it should open your mind to the possibility of having a perfect memory. This method helps you see the big picture as well as zoom in on details. It brings concepts to life and makes them concrete. Since we remember what we think about, it is always easier to remember something that you experienced in your mind.

Every memory master uses this method more than any other. It is extremely effective because you can make thousands of storage places. Think about how many markers you can make. You have visited many places in your life; you can use buildings, museums, schools, shopping malls — almost any location that you know. Make sure to choose places you know well, have significance for you, and have lots of variety. You can make routes as long as you want; you can have a place or route for every learning subject. Remember to have fun!

This system will change the way that you learn forever. The only effort will be to improve your ability to make images and place them on a familiar mental journey. It's like having crib notes or a teleprompter inside your head: The journey is like the paper, and the images are like the ink. Your imagination can attach any information to a familiar journey.

I have helped medical students, law students, pilots, managers, and business people remember all kinds of information with this method. I used it to store the first 10,000 digits of pi. A friend of mine, Dr. Yip Swee Chooi, remembered the entire Oxford English Dictionary — 1,774 pages, word for word — with this method. Anyone can store an unlimited amount of information if they choose to spend the time doing it.

Some people say, "I will run out of space."

If I gave you a truck full of objects to place in a shopping mall, would you be able to do that? Of course, you would. If you look for them, you will find thousands and thousands of places just waiting to be used in your mind. There are no limits to this system, only limits in your own thinking.

The important thing is that you practice. The more you practice, the better you will become.

14. COMMON SPEED READING MISTAKES

As we've seen, learning to read faster will save you a lot of time and help you advance in your college or professional career. When you begin learning to read faster, there are a variety of errors to avoid.

However, there are some common speed reading mistakes to avoid as you begin your studies. Here are three of the most famous blunders.

Reading All at the Same Rate

The majority of people who practice speed reading make the common error of reading all at the same speed. This is a difficult error to prevent since most speed readers direct their eyes with their hands. They end up going line-by-line at around the same pace because they're using their side, almost like they're following a beat.

Reading all at the same pace makes no sense because not everything is equally important. Some sentences and paragraphs are more critical than others, so there is no need to read them all at once. To become a more effective speed reader, you must change your reading speed according to the situation.

For optimum quality, you can change your reading speed in two ways:

- Adjusting your speed depending on the TYPE OF Content: For easy material (such as magazines), you should go faster, and for advanced material, you should go slower (i.e., textbooks). Although this seems to be self-evident, many people read it all at the same rate. This can lead to problems with comprehension. Furthermore, if you are really familiar with the material, you can try to read faster. If you aren't, go at a slower pace.
- Adjust your reading speed depending on your purpose: If your goal is simply to understand the basic concepts of the text, there is no need to read slowly. You should be pushing yourself to fly through this stuff. However, if you need a lot of information, you should probably slow down.

One of the most difficult aspects of speed reading is knowing when to accelerate and slow down. A skilled speed reader understands how to strike this balance.

Going back to re-read something when you don't have to

We've all gone back to re-read content at some stage in our lives. However, there are moments when you do not have to.

You can never return after just reading one sentence. Why is this so? While it is possible that you did not understand the sentence, isn't it also possible that the following sentence clarifies the previous one? You will not understand a sentence until you have read the rest of the paragraph.

Have you ever seen a movie that began with a very perplexing scene? Did you rewind the scene and replay it again because you didn't understand it the first time? Or did you just keep watching to find out what was going on later?

Most of the time, you're not supposed to know what's going on at the start, and the whole idea is to find it out later in the film. When you read, the same thing happens. Sometimes a sentence does not make sense until the rest of the paragraph is read.

When is it appropriate to go back and re-read something? If you've read a paragraph and still don't understand something, you should go back and read it again. Only don't do it after the first sentence.

Inadequate Concentration

To read faster, you must be able to concentrate. Regardless of your reading speed, poor concentration will wreak havoc on your comprehension. The more focused you are, the faster you can learn. Furthermore, if you can focus properly, you will comprehend the content at a faster pace.

Here are two easy ways to increase your reading focus:

- Reading with your hand aids concentration by directing your eyes around the line. You'll find that if you read with your hand or a pen as a pacer, you won't go back as often to re-read material. The easiest way to increase your reading concentration is to use your hand to direct your eyes.

- Distract yourself: Believe it or not, there are distractions that you can control. It's probably a smart idea to turn off your phone if you're trying to concentrate on your reading. Do you find yourself wanting to check your email or Facebook while reading? Then shut down your machine. If you're around people who could distract you, read somewhere else. Anticipate potential distractions and then neutralize them.

To summarize these suggestions, make sure you vary your reading pace depending on the type of material you're reading and your intended intent. Also, make sure you don't go back and re-read something you don't have to. Often, strive to increase your focus by reading with your hand and avoiding distractions. If you follow these three basic tips, you will be able to read much more quickly.

15. CONCLUSION

As a result, humans move around with two of the world's most complex structures collaborating to provide the basic foundation of knowledge through observation, thinking, writing, and, most importantly, reading.

Unfortunately, the majority of people do not take advantage of this opportunity. This is because reading is not something that arose or existed in nature. Reading is an ability that humans developed, and since humans developed it, it is not an instinctual skill that we are born with. It's a talent that needs to be mastered.

Most of us learn to read, but not all of us learn to read effectively. Our educational systems, instructors, and parents do an excellent job of teaching us how to put words together to form sentences. However, they don't always show us how to use our powerful eyes and minds most beneficially.

This could not be more untrue. We just need to learn how to use our infinitely strong eyes and minds in the right way.

This book does not involve learning or doing something new or complicated since the eyes and mind can already interpret knowledge at a high level. What it takes is a few minor changes in reading habits.

NEW GLOBE

Publishing

CPSIA information can be obtained
at www.ICGtesting.com
Printed in the USA
BVHW090930020621
608632BV00012B/244

9 781802 838596